Lalique

A collector's guide

FRONTISPIECE Eglantines (685): mirror in polished moulded glass with silvered reverse. (T3) 430mm

CHRISTOPHER VANE PERCY

Lalique

A collector's guide

CRESCENT BOOKS
New York

To Linda

Copyright © John Calmann and King Ltd, 1977

This book was designed and produced by
John Calmann and King Ltd

Library of Congress Cataloging-in-Publication Data

Percy, Christopher Vane.
    Lalique: a collector's guide/Christopher Vane Percy.
        p.   cm.
    Reprint of the Calmann & King ed.
    Bibliography: p.
    Includes index.
    ISBN 0-517-69095-0
    1. Lalique, René, 1860-1945.   2. René Lalique et cie.
3. Glassware–France–History–19th century–Collectors and
collecting.   4. Glassware–France–History–20th century–Collectors
and collecting.   I. Title.
NK5 198.L44A4   1989b
748.294–dc20   89-32305
                            CIP

This 1989 edition published by Crescent Books
distributed by Crown Publishers, Inc., 225 Park Avenue South,
New York, New York 10003.

Printed and bound in Hong Kong

ISBN 0–517–69095–0

hgfedcba

Contents

Figures at the end of each caption, T1–T11, indicate the type of trademark on the object illustrated; the key to the figures is given in Chapter 13.

1. Introduction

'LALIQUE'S GLASSWARE is commercial art perfectly conceived and realised, which permits of the introduction of a really modern and living artistic note into the decoration of our private rooms and into the arrangement and decoration of public buildings such as tearooms, hotels, cafés, dance halls, shops, banks, theatres, concert halls and so forth . . . It frankly bears the mark of our complicated civilisation, athirst for elegance, novelty, comfort and luxury.'

Gabriel Mourey's verdict, pronounced in the July 1926 issue of *Commercial Art*, was published in the wake of the 1925 Paris Exhibition and at the high tide of René Lalique's international acclaim. The coincidence was not accidental: *le style Lalique* is a natural distillation of the spirit and life-style of the twenties, borrowing from them all its most vivid and enduring qualities. In return, it provides us with a mirror of the age.

The 1925 Exhibition, the Exposition Internationale des Arts Décoratifs et Industriels Modernes, had been almost twenty years in the making. Plans to stage it in 1915 were conceived in 1907 (a significant year in the development of Lalique's career, as we shall see) and approved in 1912; they were shelved indefinitely in 1914, resurrected in 1919, then further postponed. World war and its aftermath are not conducive to the holding of international exhibitions.

By the time it was finally opened, on 28th April 1925, the Exhibition had become very largely a French affair – far more so, certainly, than the Universal Exhibition of 1900 on which its original concept had been modelled. There were no Germans and no Americans, and even the British pavilions were small and unrepresentative. It was a magnificent opportunity for French commercial artists and designers to display their skills and inventiveness – in ceramics, fashion, textiles, print and all the other decorative arts – and by so doing to resume their former pre-eminence in many of these fields.

The success with which they grasped this opportunity was destined to be brief, but while it lasted it went almost unchallenged. Its *éclat* continued to rumble around the world for the next twenty years, until war once again destroyed the society from which French designers drew their strength and inspiration.

Such was the context, frankly commercial and patriotic, in which Lalique chose to display to the world his absolute mastery of glass – its design, its manufacture and its marketing. It was a dramatic choice, perfectly timed and superbly executed; it marked the climax of his second (and greater) career, just as the Universal Exhibition of 1900 had marked the climax of his first, as a jeweller.

Those two careers were never wholly distinct. They overlapped each other in time (the watershed seems to have occurred somewhere between 1905 and 1907), and Lalique certainly applied to his glass many of the techniques which he had discovered as a jeweller. The temporal overlap was brief, however, as well as uncomfortable for him, and the technical interface was of only minor creative significance.

One essential part of Lalique's genius lay in his capacity to apply the techniques of mass production to the creation of glass objects which had hitherto been the preserve of an élite. Even if that were all, if Lalique had been no more than a highly creative and vastly successful entrepreneur, his name would still have figured prominently in the history of twentieth century glass. It would not, however, have had the special significance – almost the mystique – which it now bears; his fame would have been no less, but it would have been of a different kind and this book could not have been written.

It is to another part of Lalique's genius, less apparent and less easily defined, that this difference belongs. The magic that attaches to 'Lalique' is the same kind of magic that attaches to 'Chippendale' or 'William Morris' or 'Tiffany', or to any other such name that is identified more readily with a style than with the individual who created it. Behind all such names there lies the unique vision of one man, and the first endeavour of any collector of that man's work must be to recognise and understand his vision.

For these reasons, no purely aesthetic response to Lalique's glass – essential though that is, and instinctive though it should become – can by itself provide a sufficient basis on which to form a collection: it is also necessary to grasp something of the social, historical and technological context within which that glass was created. Much of this wider context must of necessity lie outside the scope of this book; but the collector will find its study to be amply rewarding.

My more simple object is to assist the collector to form his own judgements, based on the evidence of his eyes and on such facts of Lalique's career as seem to me to be relevant. A basic knowledge of the techniques of glass manufacture is

1. Coquilles: ceiling light in opalescent glass with satin finish and polished relief. (T3) 300mm

assumed, but I have included a chapter on Lalique's individual adaptation and refinement of those techniques, as well as a brief guide to the trademarks which can be most commonly found on his manufactured glass.

For ease of reference, if for no other reason, I have categorised Lalique's glassware by its intended use rather than by its date or style. There are in any case no distinct 'periods' for the collector to identify – even the roughest dating of Lalique's commercial output should be approached with great caution and can usually be based only on external evidence. Some of his objects, however – such as the Coquilles hanging light and fruit bowl illustrated opposite and below – were so similar in design to others whose purpose was quite different that I have thought it best to consider them together in the text, even if they were produced at entirely different dates. I also consider the distinction between Lalique's manufactured glass and his *cire perdue* objects to be essential to a proper understanding of both, and I have therefore devoted one chapter exclusively to the latter.

Figures printed in parentheses after the name of an object – e.g. Bahia (3179) – are the design numbers as they appear in the Lalique catalogue for 1932. These

2. Coupe vasque, coquilles (385): Lalique used shell designs in widely differing contexts – see the hanging light opposite. (T5) 300mm

3. René Lalique, aged about 60, at the height of his international fame

numbers, which were frequently engraved on the object, are listed in full in Chapter 14. The list will enable the collector to determine whether a particular object was made in other colours or finishes, as well as helping him to identify its name.

As I have been unable to confirm all the dimensions shown in the illustrated pages of the 1932 catalogue, I have only given those which I have either measured myself or have been able to confirm to my own satisfaction from other documentary evidence; even these may vary slightly, according to the quality of the moulding. Unless otherwise stated, dimensions given in the captions show the height of the object or, in the case of bowls and plates, its diameter. Figures from T1 to T11 at the end of each caption, before the dimension, indicate the style of the object's trademark – see Chapter 13; these styles were occasionally interchangeable, and I have only indicated those of which I have myself seen an example.

2. The man and his glass

RENÉ LALIQUE was born on 4th June 1860, at Aÿ in Champagne, the district from which his mother came and which, according to his son, Marc, inspired the appreciation of animals and the countryside which figure strongly in so much of his glass. At the age of 12 he won his first important design award at the Lycée Turgot in the Rue de Turbigo, in Paris, where he studied drawing for four years; and in 1876 he appears to have enrolled both as a student at the École des Arts Décoratifs and as an apprentice to a Paris silversmith.

In 1880, after two years of studying at a London art college, Lalique returned to Paris in order to freelance as a designer of jewels for Louis Aucoc, his former master, and for several of the world-famous firms which dominated the Paris jewelry trade. He also embarked on a number of short-lived business ventures, opening his own workshop in the Place Gaillon in 1885. It was at about this time that Lalique started seriously to explore the potential of inexpensive materials outside those traditionally used by jewellers. In 1890 he set up a small furnace to experiment with the use of glass in new premises which he had acquired in the rue Thérèse, off the Avenue de l'Opéra.

The period from 1870 to 1885 that coincided with Lalique's formative years was a time of ferment in the French decorative arts. The influence of British art in France was strong, particularly in the arts and crafts movement that developed from the work of the Pre-Raphaelites and William Morris. It was out

4. Phalènes (406): some of the butterflies are in intaglio, others are in relief on the under surface. (T3) 390 mm

of this that grew the art nouveau style in which Lalique was to complete much of his best and most famous work as a jeweller. Even painters of the French Impressionist school, which was quite different in its aims from the aesthetic movement in England, regularly visited Britain, and Monet and the Pissarros painted there frequently. One English painter, Burne-Jones, exhibited in Paris to sensational effect, and had a lasting influence on the Symbolist movement that became very important in French art at the end of the 1880s. This movement also influenced Lalique to some extent, as did the cult of Japanese design which intertwined with art nouveau and made itself felt throughout the decorative arts of Britain and France.

Throughout the nineties Lalique exhibited his own jewelry, with ever-increasing acclaim, at salons and international exhibitions all over Europe. Everywhere he collected medals almost as fast as he collected customers – Sarah Bernhardt was perhaps his most famous, Calouste Gulbenkian his richest – and in 1897 he was awarded the Croix de Chevalier de la Légion d'Honneur. By 1900, the year of the great Universal Exhibition in Paris, Lalique was among the most famous jewellers in the world; his display at that exhibition was a triumph of international dimensions. *

It was a triumph which contained within it the seeds of its own rapid decay. Already art nouveau was in decline, already Lalique and many of the more creative of his contemporaries – Léon Jallot, Maurice Dufrène, Paul Follot, André Groult – were casting around for new idioms and new materials and techniques. The results, in that first decade of the new century, were often strange.

Between about 1898 and 1906 Lalique created a number of 'important' objects which appear, in hindsight, to belong neither to his earlier work as a jeweller or to his later work as a craftsman in glass. Many were larger than life: cups and chalices the size of small fonts, made out of ivory, enamel, alabaster, glass, gold or bronze; daggers the size of swords, in rhinoceros horn or steel or silver; a huge Wagnerian peacock in enamelled metal. These were the dinosaurs of art nouveau; their natural environment lay within the glass and iron cathedrals which a previous generation had built to house its international exhibitions. Outside that environment they appeared incongruous and over-blown.

The creative significance of this curious period is difficult to assess. It was certainly not a 'fallow' period: the scale, the complexity and the sheer number of the objects which Lalique produced provide convincing evidence to the contrary. But he does appear either to have mislaid his sense of direction, or else

* In 1905 some of this jewelry was exhibited at Agnew's galleries, London. 'Thanks to René Lalique,' proclaimed the catalogue to this exhibition, 'the jeweller's art has been absolutely transformed. Before his advent, what was the jewel but a piece of vain ostentation – a braggart boast, as it were, of the possession of so much wealth? Excellent executants, whose taste was, however, limited by the requirements of industrial art, set the finest diamonds in the most dreary and monotonous of designs. The flower, the knot, the ribbon, the aigrette – do we not know them all? Small wonder that the purely aesthetic element was non-existent in settings which were at once barbarous and naive.' This extract is quoted from a long and perceptive review of the Agnew's exhibition which appeared in *The Studio* of July 1905.

5. Ambre antique, *c.* 1910, one of the earliest of the many scent bottles designed by Lalique for François Coty. 150mm

to be resting (perhaps deliberately) on the laurels which continued to shower upon him. His work at this time bears a disturbed, almost hectic quality, flaunting contrivance as a substitute for invention. By 1902 Lalique was fully installed in the extraordinary new *âtelier* – part home, part workshop, part showpiece – which he had recently designed for himself at 40 Cours la Reine (now the Cours Albert 1er), overlooking the right bank of the Seine (page 15). The quirkiness of this house, its strange failure to conform with any identifiable style of architecture, hints strongly at the disorientation which seems to have haunted all Lalique's work during these years. It was widely regarded as a 'revolutionary' house, and rightly so; but it also contained too many ghosts of earlier, outworn styles.

His break with these, and their replacement by new ideas and methods, was rapid but never, of course, complete. In 1900 Lalique was already forty, too old to shed his allegiance to the styles of his youth. He was constantly to refine and develop these styles over the next thirty or forty years, and he was to adapt them to uses of an ever increasing range and sophistication; but he never quite shook off their influence, and they can readily be identified in all but the most esoteric of his work.

Some of the scent bottles, for example, which Lalique created for François Coty well before 1910, bore the unmistakable imprint of art nouveau, both in their design and their motifs; yet they remained in production well into the thirties. Like much of Lalique's most successful work, they scarcely had time to go out of fashion (or even out of production) before they became collector's pieces, and they provide a classic example of Lalique's timeless qualities; yet they were utterly of their time, and their affinity to an art movement which was already dying when they were created is correspondingly obvious.

Not that Lalique was ever averse to invoking nostalgia for past styles, often long past. He always recognised, and often deliberately exploited, the appeal of the Antique, both in the classical motifs which he adopted (sirens, columns, shells, mythic beasts and animals) and in the care with which he would sometimes add an 'antique' patina to the surface of his wares. There was no element of fraud in this: only an astute and boldly commercial awareness that 'antiquity' is often a readily marketable commodity.

It was probably in about 1902, shortly after Lalique acquired his *âtelier* in the Cours la Reine, that he first developed an interest in the industry that was to occupy him, body and soul, for the rest of his life. The small estate which he then purchased at Clairefontaine, near Rambouillet, was almost certainly where he made the doors, panels and chandeliers for his *âtelier*; and it was probably here, in about 1907, that he first experimented with making the scent bottles for François Coty which were to become one of the most enduringly successful of all his commercial ventures. Those first bottles were manufactured elsewhere and by another company, Legras & Cie de St Denis; but two years later, when Lalique opened his second factory, at Combs-la-Ville, about forty miles east of Paris on the edge of the forest of Sénart, he was already equipped to manufacture the bottles himself. His career as *verrier* had begun.

The transition was not immediate, of course. A new shop which Lalique

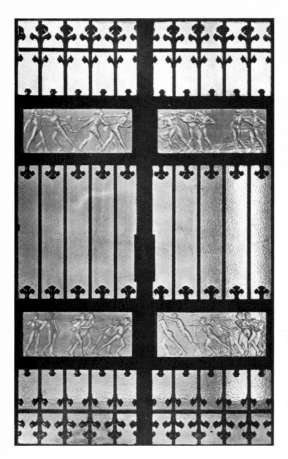

6 & 7. Photographs from a 1902 issue of *L'Illustration*, showing details from Lalique's *âtelier* in the Cours la Reine which he finished building in 1902

8. A panel from the door above

9. The *âtelier* in the Cours la Reine

opened in 1905 in the Place Vendôme was at first stocked largely with jewelry and the like – ornaments for the hair, huge pendants, boxes in silver, horn and enamel, elaborate table pieces; but the scent bottles with which he had been experimenting at Clairfontaine were already on display by 1907, and in 1911 Lalique presented what was probably the first exhibition at which his glass predominated. Invitations to this exhibition, which was staged in yet another new shop – this time in the even more fashionable Rue Royale – were sent out in the form of green glass medallions, the invitation in raised lettering on one side, a design of mistletoe on the other; it was a witty and charming device, a sign not only of Lalique's new allegiance but also of his revived capacity for innovation. The exhibition of engraved and enamelled jewelry which he presented in the following year was the last of its kind.

Lalique's work in the period immediately before the war cannot be divorced from that of his contemporaries working in other media. Emile-Jacques Ruhlmann, the great furniture designer of the twenties, held his first exhibition in 1913; Edgar Brandt exhibited his ironwork in the same year; André Groult's domestic interiors, inventive combinations of art deco and Louis XVI, were already coming into vogue, and in 1911 Maurice Marinot, later to establish himself as the master of French studio glass, forsook painting and for the first time turned his magnificent talent to glassmaking. Although Lalique was a generation older than these artists, he was still sufficiently flexible in his techniques to associate himself with their ideas and with the practical development of their careers.

It is fascinating to speculate as to the direction in which their energies would have lead these artists, and many others of similar bent, had not the first world war stemmed the creative tide into which so much of their talent had been poured. For Lalique, war meant a temporary closure of his factory; but he was soon allowed to refire his furnace in order to make laboratory equipment as part of the war effort, and in 1921, with Alsace restored to France, he bought the site for a new factory at Wingen-sur-Moder in the Bas Rhin and put his son Marc in charge of production. The show-pieces of the 1925 Paris Exhibition were created in this factory, and it became the headquarters of an industry which was to be the flag-ship of French commercial art for almost a quarter of a century; by 1926 over four hundred glass-workers were employed at the two Lalique factories.

An account of what was already known as *le style Lalique* appeared in a monograph on the artist by Gustave Geffroy in 1922, published shortly after that year's Exposition des Artistes Décorateurs in the Pavillon Marsan.* The original French is somewhat florid, and occasionally obscure, and the following is a paraphrase rather than a direct translation:

'The effect (of Lalique's stand) is at once strange and simple, bizarre and serene. Glass partitions appear to reproduce that foliage with which the winter hoar frost adorns the most ordinary of glass window-panes. . . . In the middle, a chandelier – very plain and very bold – evokes the far-off softness of a star suspended over some place of mystery. . . . Light plays the role of colour,

* *René Lalique*, Editions d'Art E. Mary (published under the direction of the Inspector of Fine Arts).

10. Advertisement, *c*. 1930, featuring the 5 Chevaux mascot (1122)

replacing it and rendering it superfluous. All the nuances which the glass assumes, all the dream-like visions which it reflects, are rigidly defined by the surrounding darkness.'

Lalique's all-pervasive presence at the 1925 Exhibition is described in Chapter 9 of this book. After that date there are few major landmarks, only a dazzling progress from one grand architectural commission to the next, a steadily wider and more sophisticated range of commercial production, and the creation of those one-off masterpieces in *cire perdue* which can convert the collection of Lalique glass from a largely academic exercise, however rewarding, into a joyous treasure hunt.

In 1928 the Breves Galleries in Basil Street, Knightsbridge, took over from Edward Trower and Co. as Lalique's agents for Britain and the Empire, devoting one of their first-floor showrooms to a permanent display of his glass against a background in the Chinese style. Breves catalogues and leaflets over the next

THE VERY LATEST DESIGNS

SPIRIT OF THE WIND

| For light | £7 | 17 | 6 |
| Unilluminated | £6 | 16 | 6 |

FROG

| For light | £3 | 13 | 6 |
| Unilluminated | £2 | 12 | 6 |

WEEPING SIREN

| For light | £5 | 5 | 0 |
| Unilluminated | £4 | 4 | 0 |

PEACOCK

| For light | £5 | 5 | 0 |
| Unilluminated | £4 | 4 | 0 |

The above are post free in British Isles only

11. Advertisement, *c.* 1930; the designs are Nos. 1103, 832, 1140, and 1146

few years provide a valuable indication of the range of objects that were by now available to the British public, including the car mascots which they began to promote in Britain in 1930. When Breves opened new premises, in September 1933, the occasion was honoured by a number of dignitaries, French and British, and the 73 year old designer himself paid a flying visit. He was held up at the last minute by the sudden death of a senior colleague, and arrived in Bond Street almost one and a half hours late for the opening ceremony. The consequences were recorded by a reporter from *The Manchester Guardian*:

'At one time his arrival seemed so unlikely that the Mayor of Westminster and M. Corbin, the French Ambassador, made their speeches in his praise. Half an hour later, after they and Lady Oxford, Princess Bibesco, and the other distinguished guests had left, M. Lalique, a little white-haired man, with a white tie and an enormous brown overcoat, drew up in his car from Croydon. In his short look round the exhibits he did nothing to belie his reputation of being one of the shyest men in France, in spite of a somewhat brisk military appearance, suggestive of Cheltenham rather than the Champs Elysées.'

A reporter from *The Times* was also there, and took the opportunity both to describe the new gallery and to record some pertinent views of his own as to the quality of the glass displayed:

'Whether it be liked or not, the ornamental glass associated with the name of M. René Lalique deserves recognition as the first attempt in Europe to explore the full possibilities of glass as a plastic material, and Messrs. Breves, its agents in London, are to be congratulated on the general effect of their new galleries. A plain shopfront faced with travertine, with the name in white metal above, opens to a deeply recessed window which allows a clear view of the whole interior. As far as is possible all the working features, such as doors, and the decorations of the new galleries are constructed of Lalique glass, in association with stainless steel, and this concentration upon the substance to be sold is a good example, as contributing to unity of effect.

'The general background for the glass is warm neutral – brown carpets, walnut veneers to the showcases, and brown walls below, paling to broken ivory in the ceiling. Some elaborate examples of M. Lalique's art – tables, doors, and panels – are shown, but one's preference is for the simpler pieces, the table glass in particular. A development which deserves encouragement is the increase in designs which can be multiplied. Not only is the demand for "unique" pieces almost purely snobbish, but their production gives a pretext for the elaborate modelling which alienates artistic sympathy from the glass. In this case, as in so many others, a forced limitation of design produces good results, and some of the table glass is quite beautiful.'

Also in 1933, the Musée des Arts Décoratifs mounted a retrospective exhibition representing all of Lalique's work over the past fifty years – jewelry, *objets d'art*, sculptures, paintings and the entire range of his glass, from the early years of the century up to his latest religious works. Such an exhibition, mounted in the artist's own life-time, was an exceptional honour, and it pin-points the climax of Lalique's career.

Demand for Lalique's commercial output, most of it designed in the early twenties, declined perceptibly in the years immediately prior to the second world war, and in 1937 the factory at Combs-la-Ville was closed. Lalique's esteem was undiminished, however, and when the newly crowned King George VI and Queen Elizabeth paid a state visit to France in 1938 the Conseil Municipal de Paris presented them with four candlesticks and a vast dinner service designed by him, consisting of twelve settings of four sizes of wine glasses with matching dessert plates, and a Caravelle *surtout*. The plates were engraved with two coats of Arms, the City of Paris and the House of Windsor, and the stems of the glasses bore a seagull motif which co-ordinated with the *surtout*. It was a magnificent gift, as sincere a tribute to René Lalique as to their Majesties.

Two years later the Germans re-occupied Alsace. Lalique was forced to close his last remaining factory, which was severely damaged during the war; but by 1951, when an exhibition of the art of glass was staged at the Pavillon de Marsan, Marc Lalique had already reconstructed it and restored its furnaces to

12. Candlestick from the dinner service presented by the city of Paris to King George VI and Queen Elizabeth in 1938

production; a huge chandelier which Marc designed for the 1951 exhibition now hangs in the entrance hall to the Musée des Arts Décoratifs.

Shortly after René Lalique's death, on 5th May 1945, Calouste Gulbenkian sent a letter to his daughter, Suzanne. 'Your father,' he wrote, 'was a very cherished friend, and the grief attendant on his death is heightened by the infinite sorrow one always feels at the loss of a great man. My admiration for his unique *oeuvre* has never ceased to grow throughout the fifty years of our friendship, and I feel, I am absolutely convinced, that full justice has not been done him yet. He ranks amongst the greatest figures in the history of Art of all time, and his so personal masterly touch, his exquisite imagination, will excite the admiration of future élites.'

13. Suzanne (833): satin finish. (T2) 230mm

3. For the collector

FIFTEEN YEARS AGO, Lalique glass existed only in the homes of connoisseurs or of those who had acquired it when new, in a few widely scattered museums*, and in French flea markets or English jumble sales. All that has changed and the dramatic revival in the appreciation of Lalique over recent years has created a new and often unpredictable market, with few rules and plenty of exceptions. My own experience of the market, both as a collector and as a dealer, began in about 1970 and may therefore be of interest to those intending to start or expand collections of their own.

It was not until 1974 that I first realised quite how widely popular Lalique glass had suddenly become. In the autumn of that year my wife and I assembled our own collection, together with a number of items on loan and for sale, in order to stage the world's first post-war exhibition of Lalique glass at our gallery in Weighhouse Street, London. Its success was astonishing to us both: planned to finish after six weeks, it lasted six months, and people flocked to see it from all walks of life and from all over Europe and America. Among our earliest visitors from Paris were Lalique's son and grand-daughter, Marc and Marie-Claude, and we were delighted to hear from Marc that he believed it to be the most comprehensive assembly of his father's work to have been exhibited since before the war. †

In 1969 it was perfectly possible for the collector to acquire one of Lalique's most popular statuettes, Suzanne (833), for about £10 from a dealer who might himself have bought it at a jumble sale for a few pre-decimalisation shillings. Over the next three or four years the rise in prices was slow, for the collector knew that more and more pieces were coming on to the market, and that he might well find an identical statuette more cheaply.

By 1973, however, that same Suzanne could have realised £100 – more, if it still had its original bronze base. My own collection by this time had reached about eighty pieces, most of which I had selected from the stock which my wife and I had been acquiring since 1970 for our London gallery. In the summer of 1974, almost overnight, auction prices of five years ago and less were being doubled; it cost me £200 to replace a Deux sauterelles vase (915) which I had sold only months previously for £90. A Victoire car mascot (1147) had already fetched £600 in 1973, and Suzanne statuettes were fetching up to £300.

I mention these facts only to record this first astonishing upsurge. Prices have levelled out somewhat since then, and although they will probably continue to

---

* Even today the museums which house significant collections of Lalique are few and far between. The chief ones are the Musée des Arts Décoratifs in Paris, the Calouste Gulbenkian Museum in Lisbon, and, thanks to the recent generosity of Mr Martin Battersby, the Brighton Museum in Britain. There are also two interesting collections in the United States – the Toledo Museum and the Corning Museum in New York.

† Eight pieces from this collection were photographed for inclusion in their *Lalique par Lalique*, published by Edipop of Lausanne in 1977.

rise, in tune with those of other established markets, a clearer pattern of pricing for each object in the Lalique range is likely to become evident as the years go by.

Meanwhile, it becomes increasingly important for the would-be collector to know his subject and to recognise individual items for what they are. The period during which Lalique manufactured his glass was so long, and his output was so vast and varied, that the chances of lighting upon a design or a colour for the first time are still quite high; and there is the additional pleasure of discovering differences in quality between apparently identical pieces.

One of the most significant of these differences, the quality of the moulding, is easy to account for. A model such as the Formose vase (934) was shown at the 1925 Exhibition and was still in production ten years later; during that period the moulds would have been replaced many times, and the definition of the moulding would alter accordingly. There may be other variations, too – not all of them so readily perceptible; not only was the Formose vase produced in a number of different colours – red, green and yellow as well as clear – but even the clear variety could range from a white and chilly transparency to a soft and (for some) more appealing warmth, sometimes with the added luxury of hand-tinting. It could also be opalescent, sometimes but not always glowing beautifully when held under light. Colours might vary in strength, and even the weight of the vase could change according to the efficiency with which the glass had been blown into the mould.

Similar criteria can usually be applied to other ranges. I was fortunate enough to have the chance of comparing four examples of a Tête d'aigle mascot (1138)

14. Tête d'aigle (1138): the glass has an amethyst hue with satin finish and polished relief. (T8) 61mm

15. Black and clear glass versions of the Tête d'aigle seal (175), probably designed before the first world war. (T2) 78mm

which was probably first promoted as such in 1927 and varied considerably in quality over the years. One was in clear, very white glass, badly polished with rough acided feathers and little definition; another was of a warm, clear natural colour, with a soft-textured acid finish and a subtle polish on its raised surfaces; the third was of a slightly amethyst hue, only perceptible in comparison with the first; and the fourth, acided and with a tint of topaz, was subtly polished on all its raised surfaces, giving beautiful definition to the feathers and a patinated surface. The dimensions of all four were slightly different, both in height and width.

No matter what the quality, however, the collector will always be well advised to acquire one example of any model. Chances of finding another and better one will become increasingly rare, and it should prove possible, over the

years, to improve any collection by means of an exchange for a similar piece. The collector should also bear in mind that single items which once belonged to a set, or even merely to a pair, tend to be over-priced; this applies in particular to items of tableware, especially dinner services.

Finally, one must beware of the myths which all too often gather around a particular item, and seldom bear much relation to the truth. Of these, the most common and most misleading is that of the 'signed piece': however applied, the name 'Lalique' or the several variations thereof (see Chapter 13) is never more than a trademark. Only in the rarest instances did Lalique personally sign even his *cire perdue* objects, and then only by scratching his name into the wax

16. Formose (934): a popular vase displayed at the 1925 Exhibition, available in many colours. (T6) 180mm

17. OPPOSITE Papillons (2650): scent burner with detachable top in satin glass with butterflies in polished relief. (T2) 200mm

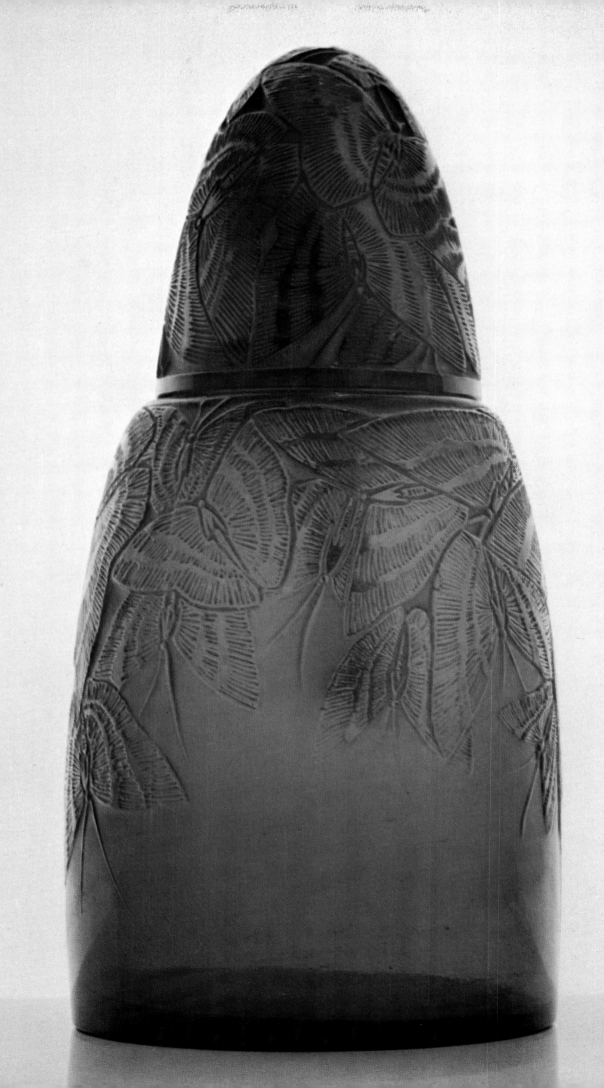

18. Vase with a geometrical design, typical of Lalique's work in the mid-thirties. Only its plain base distinguishes it from a ceiling lamp-shade decorated in an identical style. (T8) 330mm

immediately before casting.* In any case, the commercial value attaching to such a 'signature', as well as being spurious, is based on a serious misconception. Many of Lalique's finest creations were manufactured in vast quantities, yet most of them possess the singular, 'one-off' quality which is normally associated with the most exclusive studio work. That is the essence of their appeal, and if the collector does not respond to it he has failed to understand the most vital aspect of Lalique's genius.

Another kind of myth, equally misleading but far harder to disprove, relates to the purported ownership of an object which might otherwise be quite commonplace: there would sometimes appear to be more Lalique car mascots that 'once belonged to a high-ranking Nazi officer' than there were Corporals in the entire German Army. Precious few pieces specially made by Lalique for Royalty or famous actresses or for a member of his own family ever come on to the market. Collectors should treat such claims with extreme caution. They should remember too, that although it has long been too expensive to manufacture opalescent glass on a commercial scale (and that therefore any such pieces, whether from the Lalique factory or any other, are almost certain to be pre-1940) the process was certainly not Lalique's invention, nor did it die with him.

In 1946, when Marc Lalique re-started his father's company as Cristal Lalique, the initial R was dropped from the factory's trademarks. A few pre-war designs continued in production, however, and some of these retained their trademarks in exactly the original form. It is therefore incorrect to assume that all objects marked 'R. Lalique', in whatever form, were produced before the war, and the collector will only learn to distinguish between the two periods from his own observation and experience. Pre-war designs produced since 1946 tend to be white and crisp in appearance, and to lack some of the warmth and subtlety associated with Lalique production in the thirties. None have been produced in opalescent or coloured glass, enamelling is rare, and hand-staining has ceased altogether. If the glass in question is coloured or has an amethyst or champagne tint, or if its surface is enamelled, stained or patinated, it is safe to assume that it was both produced and designed before 1940.

Lalique had several imitators – Sabino, Eteling, Genet et Michon and André Hunebelle all produced glass of a more or less similar style and quality – but I am unaware of any deliberate forgeries, and no very deep knowledge is required to distinguish the genuine article from its imitations. Almost every piece produced by the Lalique factories bears a trademark (see Chapter 13) and many bear a design number in addition (Chapter 14); but the perceptive collector will soon learn to recognize the master's work without requiring confirmation of this kind.

---

* Occasionally, either at the special request of the purchaser or because the moulded or sand-blasted trademark was in capital letters, an item would be sent back to the factory to have a script 'signature' added. Such items, bearing two styles of trademark, are no more 'personal' to Lalique than any others.

BETWEEN 1920 AND 1930 Lalique designed more than 200 vases and 150 bowls, and although by the time the 1932 catalogue was published at least 50 of the vases had been discontinued, presumably for commercial reasons, these two categories are still the most readily available as well as the most interesting for the Lalique collector today. Lalique was himself particularly proud of his vases, designing them as objects for display and for the kind of aesthetic appreciation more commonly reserved for antique or studio glass. They were not

19. OPPOSITE Bacchantes (997): a brilliant use of high relief to convey movement and sensuality. This vase is still made by Cristal Lalique. (T1) 250mm

20. One of Lalique's earliest vases: opaque and heavily stained in sea-green, it was briefly revived by Cristal Lalique after the second world war. (T5) 270mm

21. Martigues (377): opalescent bowl supported from below by the fins of the three central fish. (T8) 365mm

22. Detail of plate 21

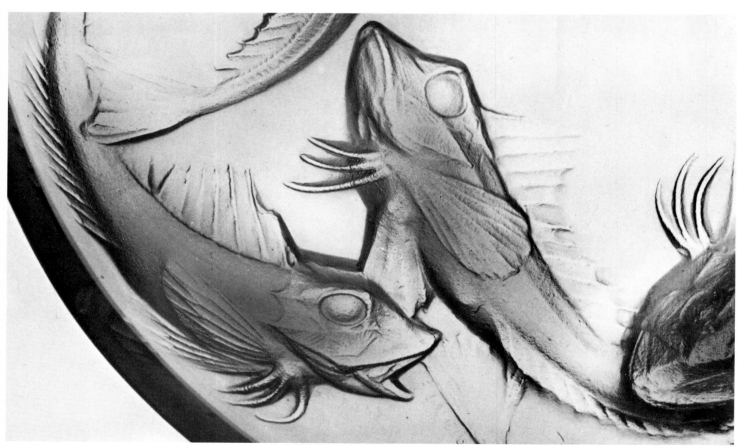

23. Gui (948): satin base with a slight polish on the leaves and berries of the mistletoe. (T2) 170mm

intentionally designed 'to put things in', and although they sometimes lend themselves to flower arrangement, the modern collector's first priority should be to display them in an appropriate setting.

Certain vases – Pétrarque (1024) for instance, with its massive handles of thick glass – stand very well by themselves, while smaller groups of similar theme or colour – such as Formose (934) and Salmonides (1015) – may be happily grouped together; coordination of this kind is an exciting and rewarding method of collection.

24. OPPOSITE Moissac (992): vase with unusual gun-metal colour and satin finish. (T1) Approximately 200mm

25. Milky, opaque vase with traces of hand-tinting. (T2) 233mm

26. Druides (937): opalescent vase, slightly stained blue-grey; the berries are polished. (T2) 175mm

Almost all Lalique's vases were produced in either clear or opalescent glass; most were available in coloured glass as well – a marvellously coiled Serpent (896) in amber, Druides (937) in emerald green mistletoe, and Courges (900), a pumpkin design in pale amethyst, are three striking examples; but these seem to have been less popular than the typical 'Lalique' opalescent models, and they are correspondingly rare today. Other such rarities include two bronze-handled vases, Cluny (961) and Senlis (962), while vases and bowls with a silver band running round the rim, such as Moissac (992) or Tournon (401) are more common.

27. ABOVE Petrarque (1024): the 20mm thick body is satin glass and the relief on the handles is highly polished. (TI) 220mm

28. BELOW Pierrefonds (990): white glass with satin body and polished handles. (TI) 153mm

29. ABOVE Eucalyptus (936): a heavily moulded vase in satin white glass. (T1) 165mm

30. OPPOSITE Rampillon (991): a small opalescent vase with a hand-stained floral design. (T3) 126mm

The heavier and more solid vases with open tops such as Pierrefonds (990) with its huge open-scrolled glass handles or Rampillon (991) with its raised diamond design, were generally made in the power press. Lighter or thinner vases with restricted tops – such as Sophora (977) or Gui (948) were made by blowing the glass into moulds.

Lalique showed several of his finest vases – among them Tourbillons (973), Chamaraude (974), Ornis (976) and Charmilles (978) – at the 10th Exhibition of Contemporary French Craftsmen in November 1926, reviewed and illustrated in the January 1927 issue of *Mobilier et Décoration*, the leading French magazine on the decorative arts: 'One discovers,' wrote Gabriel Henriot, Librarian of the Bibliothèque Forney, 'all (Lalique's) precious talents; refined taste, good material, excellent proportions and purity of line, perfection in the grace of his curves . . . What a wonderful material is glass, full of joy, full of light, lending itself perfectly to the art of decoration: rustic plants or watery algae, birds of the sky or fish of the moving oceans, human beings or mythological monsters, it is a

31. Tourbillons (973): heavily moulded vase with enamelled high relief. (T1) 200mm

32. Small, highly polished vase with a brown stained background. (TI) 186mm

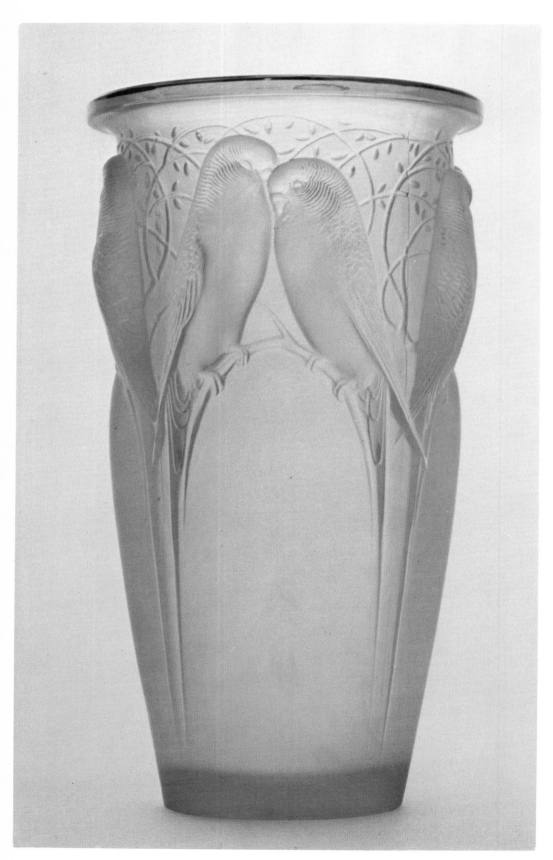

33. Ceylan (905): pairs of birds in lightly polished relief against a satin background. (T3) 240mm

34. OPPOSITE Coqs et plumes (1033): polished design of cockerels in high relief against a tinted satin background. (T1) 155mm

35. A monumental vase, blown into a vast mould, perhaps with the aid of compressed air. (T5). 420mm

36. Danaïdes (972): the pouring water is polished in contrast with the satin background. (T8) 180mm

37. Archers (893): polished relief against satin background. (T6) 240mm

38. *Top left* Coupe Chicorée (3213): salad bowl in white glass with satin relief. (T1) 235mm; *Bottom left* Fruit bowl in frosted glass with polished base. (T1) 240mm; *Right* Clear glass salad bowl with dandelion design in satin finish. (T3) 235mm

poem which sings at each stroke of the beautifully formed glass – for example on the side of a beautiful vase where the decoration stands strongly in relief on the thick glass, which protects its limpid qualities and enriches its precious lustre.'

Bowls, also usually opalescent and second only to vases in their current popularity with collectors, were designed by Lalique both as individual items and as sets – e.g. Chicorée (3213) is particularly attractive – were designed as accessories to Lalique's tableware; others were simply ornaments; but the vast majority were intended for use, either for fruit or salads or flowers. By the early thirties they had become widely popular as gifts, for they were usually less expensive than vases and their functional qualities provided the middle classes with a flimsy but useful excuse for purchasing an apparent extravagance.

Some of the later bowls, it must be admitted, were as commercial in their design as they were in manufacture, and in contrast to almost all Lalique's vases carry a cheap, almost plastic appearance, more appropriate to the thirties than the twenties. One of the most frequently found designs in this category depicts a whirlpool of bubbles and fishes; it can be found in at least three shapes – as a shallow bowl, as a steep-sided bowl and as a plate – and all three were manufactured in two sizes. Far more impressive, to my eye, and of much greater interest to the collector, is the stylish Eléphants (411); and the monkeys shown in high relief round the rim of the satin-glass Madagascar (403) are particularly attractive.

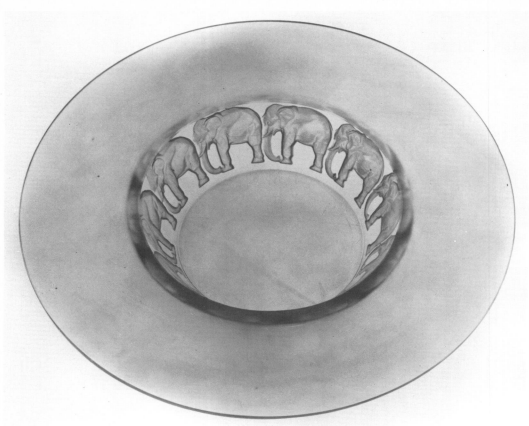

39. Eléphants (411): the animals are in intaglio on clear glass and the brim is satin. (T3) 385mm

40. Detail of plate 39

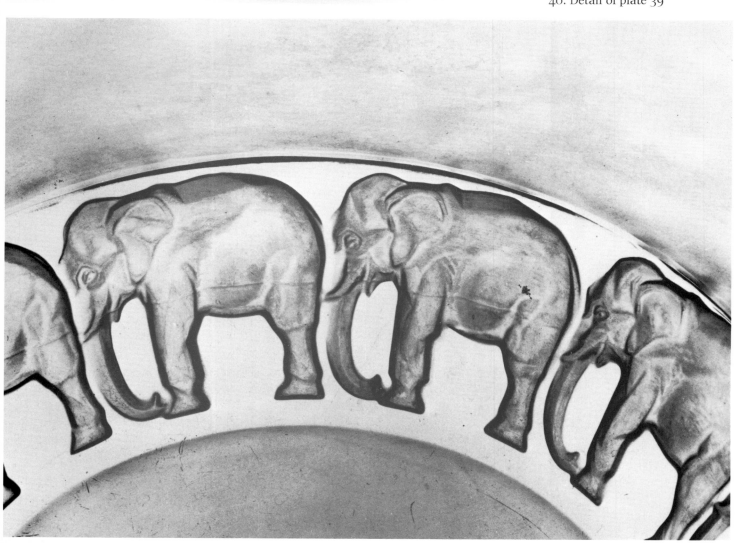

41. Madagascar (403): in
opalescent, satin glass with
masks in high relief. (T9) 300mm

42. Detail of plate 41

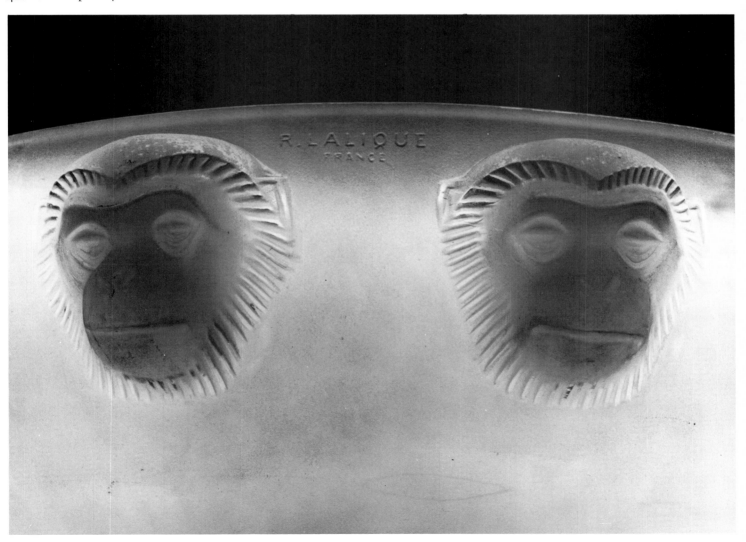

43. A completely clear vase designed to complement a dinner service. (T8) 165mm

44. Spirales (1060): opalescent vase with blue staining on the raised relief against a satin background. (TI) 240mm

45. Prunes (1037): the thick relief is in satin with polished highlights. (TI) 175mm

46. Cerises (1035): presented in 1977 to Princess Grace of Monaco. 200mm

OPPOSITE
47. ABOVE LEFT Heavy vase with a pattern of stylized flowers against background of crushed ice. (TI) 183mm

48. ABOVE RIGHT Heavy moulded vase with a wave design in polished relief against background of crushed ice. (TI) 160mm

49. BELOW LEFT Ferrières (1019): opalescent, with a polished relief against a greeny-blue satin background. (T2) 170mm

50. BELOW RIGHT Highly polished opalescent vase with a design of petals. (TI) 250mm

51. Tournai (956): satin background with leaves in polished relief. (T6) 120mm

52. Covered vase with satin finish and a border of devil masks round the neck. (TI) approximately 200mm

53. Amiens (1023): a clear glass vase with handles in a satin finish. (T8) 180mm

54. Chamaraude (974): clear, slightly topaz body, with brown staining on the satin handles. (T3) 195mm

55. Honfleur (994): a small, fine vase with lightly stained handles. (T3) 141mm

56. Ornis (976): wide variations in thickness give the base and birds an opalescent appearance. (T3) 170mm

57. Béliers (904): polished glass with satin handles. (T3) 185mm

58. Fruit bowl in white glass, hand-stained in green. (TI) 244mm

59. Marguerite: the flowers are clear, in contrast to a greeny-blue background. (TI) 335mm

60. Dahlias (938): satin white
glass with enamelled stamens.
(T2) 140mm

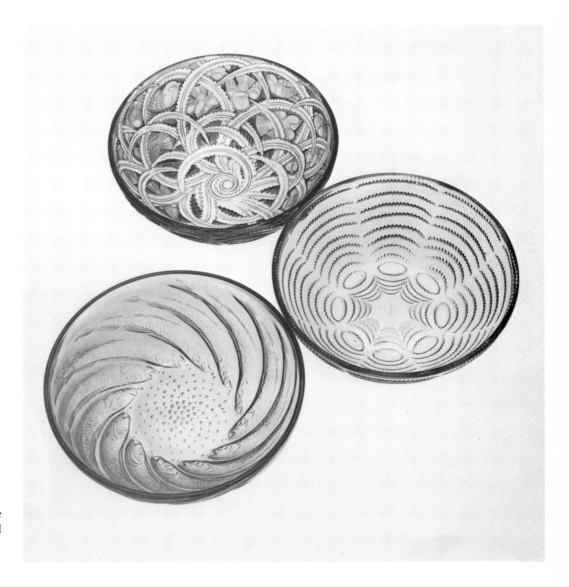

61. Three fruit bowls: the fish
design (T9) is opalescent, the
moulded chaffinches (T1) are pale
blue and the stylized thirties bowl
(T1) is in clear glass. 240mm,
235mm, 235mm

62. Poissons (925): opaque and lightly polished, with a satin tinted background. (T4) 235mm

63. Brilliant blue bowl with a design of peacock feathers. (T9) 300mm

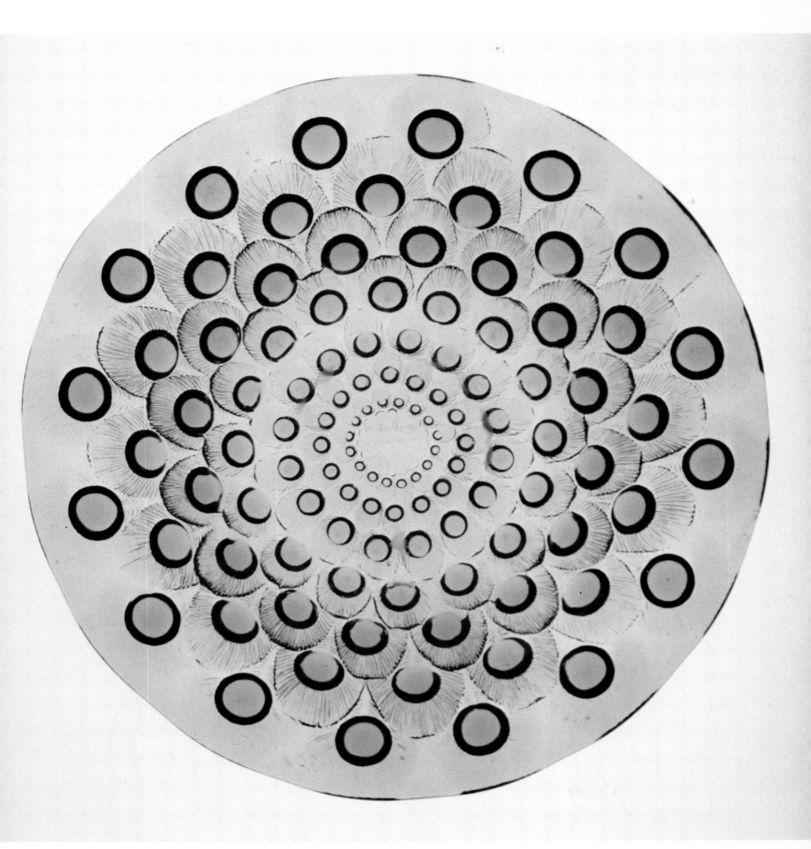

64. Sophora (977): polished relief on a satin background. (T6) 250mm

5. Tableware

FOR ALMOST TWO DECADES, from the early twenties until the end of the thirties, tableware by Lalique featured prominently among the presents at middle-class weddings in London, Paris, Melbourne and Cape Town. Lalique's vast output in this field provided the foundation for his success in the mass market, and it is also the source of an apparently inexhaustible supply of acquisitions for the modern collector. Sets of Lalique wine glasses, tumblers, fruit plates and salad bowls are still to be found all over the world.

65. *Left* Verres Nippon (5244): two wine glasses from an extensive range of tableware. (T11) 77mm; *Right* A decanter in polished glass, stopper with satin finish and polished relief. (T4) 135mm

In the France of the mid-twenties, however, such items still carried the ultra-fashionable cachet – *très snob, presque cad* – which was reflected at its most dramatic in the marble dining room designed by Lalique for the Sèvres porcelain company at the 1925 Exhibition. Had the Sèvres plates been removed from the table and replaced by dessert plates to match the wine glasses and decanter, the entire setting would have been by Lalique: it was displayed against a 'tapestry' in beige marble, heavily veined in grey, depicting a boar hunt; the table itself was by Lalique, and above it floated a coffered glass ceiling (also by Lalique) lit from within and mirrored by the patterned marble floor. However unsatisfactory the room's acoustics, the visual effect was dazzling and monumental; it was far grander, and hence less overtly commercial, than the equally monumental dining room which Lalique designed for his own pavilion at the same exhibition.

Three years later, to judge by the Breves catalogue of 1928, any well-to-do British hostess could have given a Lalique dinner party, had she been so inclined. Imagine the scene: cocktails before dinner, poured out of a Lalique

66. Artist's impression of the dining room in the Lalique pavilion at the 1925 Exposition des Arts Décoratifs

BG.

67. A decanter and one of four different sizes of wine glass from a set designed in the late twenties. (TII) 255mm. (TII) 135mm

68. Bourgueil: decanter and glasses in clear glass with relief in satin finish; this set was first made after 1932 and has been continued by Cristal Lalique. (TI) Jug, 230mm. Large glass, 135mm. Medium-sized glass, 111mm. Small glass, 95mm

69. OVERLEAF LEFT White glass decanter, part of a set designed before 1925. (T8) 200mm

70. OVERLEAF RIGHT Attractive decanter, part of a set, in clear moulded glass with a border round the neck in a satin finish. (T8) 300mm

71 & 72. Tableware presented by the city of Paris to King George VI and Queen Elizabeth in 1938

73. Dinner plate from the same service. The coats of Arms are those of the House of Windsor and the City of Paris

carafe into Lalique tumblers; cigarettes offered from a Lalique *bôite*, its matching ashtray resting on a small mahogany table inset with a glass panel by Lalique. Later, each guest will be seated in front of a place-card gripped in a Lalique holder, studying a menu card set in the same fashion and toying with a Lalique wine glass (four sizes at each setting); the room will be lit during dinner by a pair of Lalique candelabra on the table and a large overhead bowl with matching wall brackets, also by Lalique; hors d'oeuvres and sauces, salads and desserts, fruit and cheese – all will be served in Lalique bowls or on Lalique plates; by every guest will be a Lalique finger bowl, and the champagne glasses (by Lalique – who else?) will each hold a matching swizzle stick. Over the port, or rather under it, there will be the discreet glow of the Lalique table, illuminated from beneath.

It is in this broad category that the collector is likely to find more items than in any other. Complete sets or services are almost unprocurable, owing to breakages (these items were, after all, *used*) and the natural propensity of dealers and auctioneers to split the few complete sets which do reach the market. The collector will soon also come to recognise that certain designs of tableware were

74. A lemonade set in amber glass. (TI). Jug, 225mm. Glasses, 125mm

75. Jaffa (3176): a white glass lemonade set with satin finish. (TI). Jug, 225mm. Glasses, 125mm. Tray, approximately 450mm

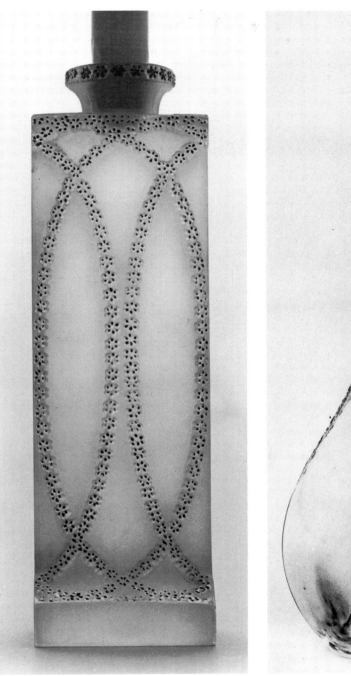

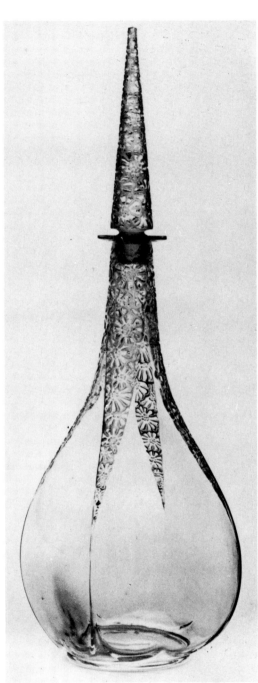

76. LEFT Candlestick in frosted glass with flowers in gold enamel. (T8) 220mm

77. RIGHT Marguerites (3161): white glass carafe with satin design. (T4) 360mm

far more popular than others: the opalescent Coquilles bowl (385), for instance, is a common find today; so is the fine Sirènes bowl (375) which, even in 1932, cost over 2,000 francs (about £21 or $75). A set of four glasses or a pair of plates are well worth collecting, but fruit bowls or dishes produced as single items are preferable. It is possible to build up larger sets, particularly of glasses, but great care is required to guard against differences in colour, however slight. Such differences will be less apparent, and are less important, in the case of patinated glasses or tumblers, such as Bahia (3179).

78. Set of tableware in clear glass with green staining on the satin relief. (T1). Decanter, 280mm. Jug, 210mm. Glasses, 110mm

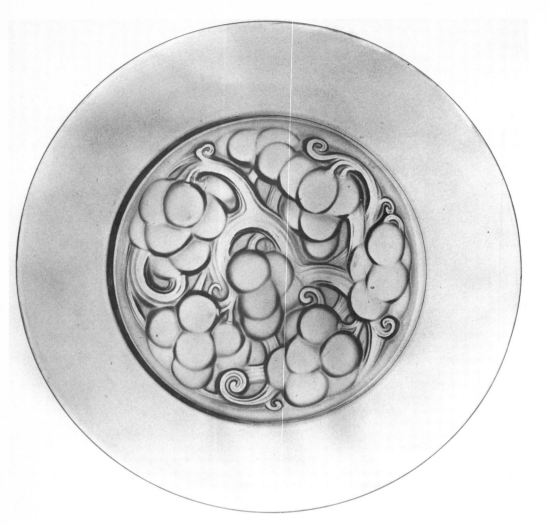

79. Marienthal: plate in white frosted glass. (T8) 214mm

80. A white glass bowl with frosted border showing traces of blue staining. (TI) 300mm

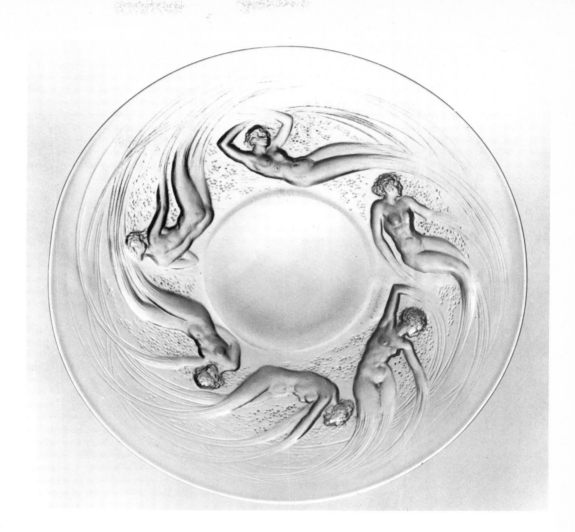

81. Ondines (3003): white glass
with frosted relief. (T3) 207mm

82. Lys (382): clear glass body supported by opalescent lilies. (T3) 210mm

83. Archer (1126): car mascot in
clear glass with satin-finished
intaglio design. (T6) 130mm

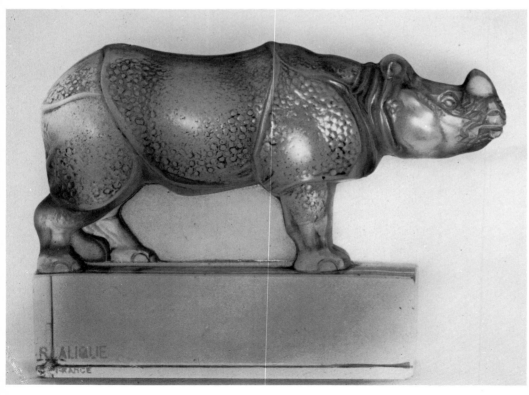

84. Rhinocéros (1195): satin
finish with grey hand-staining on
a clear glass base. (T1) 90mm

CAR MASCOTS, most of them originally designed as paper-weights, are the most widely prized of all Lalique objects. Attracting motor enthusiasts as well as Lalique collectors, they have acquired a mystique that seems quite unrelated to their aesthetic qualities and has produced a largely artificial market. It is none the less real for that, however, and no dealer or collector can afford to ignore it.

A few words, first, about the comparatively rare paper-weights which were manufactured and remained as such – either because their bases were obviously unsuitable for conversion into car mascots or merely because no motorist thought to do so. These light little objects (they should not be used to hold down anything heavier than a postage stamp, and sometimes even their balance is unreliable) were clearly intended to be decorative rather than practical; but Lalique excelled himself in providing each one of them with a personality of its

85. 5 Chevaux (1122): a car mascot commissioned by Citroën in 1925. (T6) 110mm

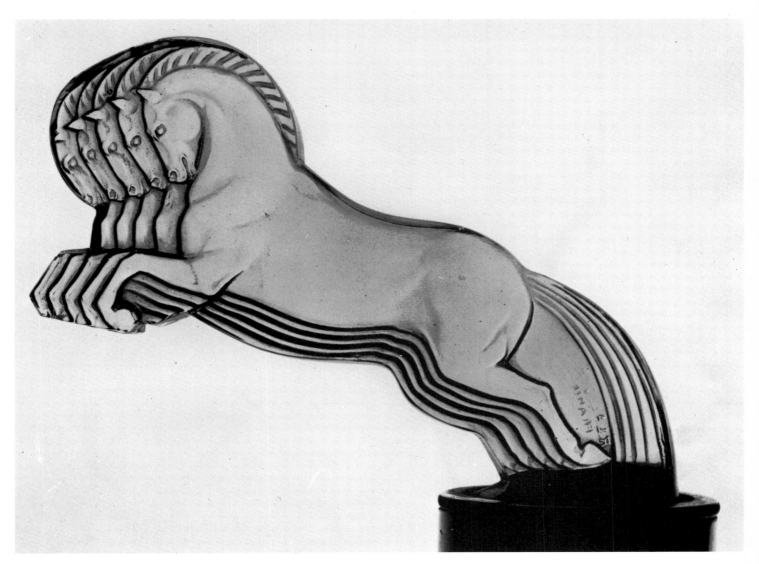

86. LEFT Aigle (428): white glass with satin finish and traces of grey staining. (T4) 222mm
87. RIGHT Faucon (1124): polished clear glass. (T8) 190mm

own, and the collector will find that they blend perfectly either with other Lalique items or, indeed, with *objets d'art* of other periods. One of the largest, Deux aigles (801), conveys an antique, almost classical quality; the clear glass Eléphant (1191) or Rhinocéros (1195), on the other hand, are of a modern form and provide realistic representations of their subjects.

Although there is evidence that a few Lalique paper-weights may have been adapted as car mascots during the first world war, it was not until about 1925 that Citroën commissioned the famous 5 Chevaux (1122) for their 5CV model; and it was another two years before Lalique started to promote mascots as a commercial venture. The mascot prices of 1927 seem more ridiculously low today than those for almost any other category of Lalique. They ranged from 10s. 6d. for an Archer (1126) on a standard chrome base to four guineas for a coloured Tête de paon (1140) on a specially commissioned base: Lalique was probably unsure of the demand, and priced his mascots accordingly. At the Paris Motor Salon of 1928, however, that great status symbol, the Minerva, was displayed sporting a Victoire (1147), and it is clear that the public rapidly became fascinated by the idea; by 1931 Lalique mascots were sufficiently well established for a writer in *The Studio* to refer to them as 'essentially an item of *décor*, as much so as a glittering ornament in a lady's hat.'

Exceptionally, the Victoire, the 5 Chevaux and a few other models – they include the Vitesse (1160), the Epsom (1153) and the Comète (1123) – were

88. Hirondelle (1143): polished
clear glass with satin base. (T8)
150mm

89. Comète (1123): clear glass.
(T8) 185mm long

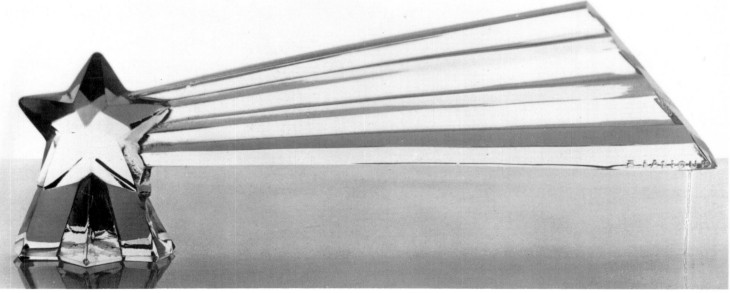

92. OPPOSITE Tête de paon (1140): car mascot on part of its original chromium-plated base. (T6) 177mm

90. LEFT Grande libellule (1145): car mascot with satin-finished body and polished relief and wings. (T4) 110mm

91. BELOW Epsom (1153): car mascot in white glass with satin finish and polished mane. (T8) 182mm

initially designed as mascots; it is therefore unusual to find these models damaged as a result of efforts to fix them to a base. Most of the other models, however, shared the dual role of paper-weight and mascot, and in some cases such damage was inevitable; the claws of Coq nain (1135) and Hirondelle (1143) were particularly vulnerable in this respect, and it seems strange that Lalique did not see fit to provide them with specially moulded bases, as he did in the case of Chrysis (1183). At least one model, Faucon (1124), seems to have been specially designed to serve both purposes.

There were several types of base available, both in Britain and in France: simple chrome collars that fixed directly onto the car, bases which incorporated an electric light and a choice of colour filters (see plate 101), even an electrified base which contained a revolving disc and made the larger version of Libellule (1145) seem to flap its wings at a speed corresponding to that of the car. One of the reasons for such a variety was that the Lalique shop in Paris did not export bases, and overseas agents were left to supply their own; Breves even went so far

93. Grenouille (1146): car mascot, on its original chromium-plated base (engraved 'Breves Gallery'), in clear glass with satin and polished finish. (T8) 160mm

94. Coq nain (1135): dark grey polished glass with blood red centre. (T8) 205mm

95. Victoire (1147): satin finish with the stylized hair polished; the glass has an amethyst hue. (T8) 265mm

97. Deux aigles (801): satin finish with blue staining and polished relief and base. (T1) 80mm

96. Sanglier (1157): dark grey, satin finished glass with polished features and base. (TI) 95mm

98. Chrysis (1183): white glass with satin finish. (TI) 135mm

99. Saint-Christophe (1142): car mascot in clear glass with satin-finished intaglio design. (T6) 130mm

100. Petite libellule (1144): white glass with satin finish and polished relief. (T7) 162mm

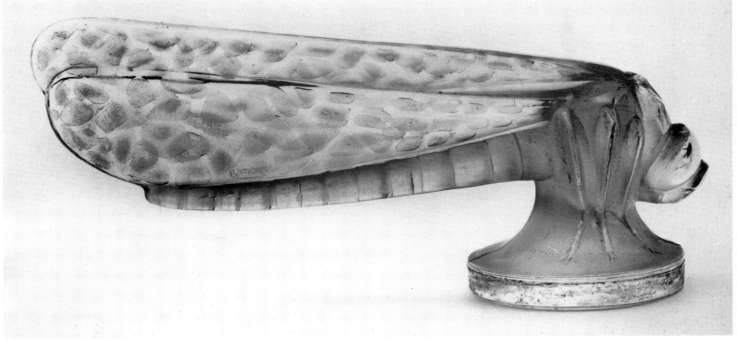

as to stamp theirs with their own name and address. Some of these original bases can still be found, occasionally still attached to their original mascot, and the value of both is correspondingly increased. Most bases, however, were interchangeable.

Most models, whether mascot or paper-weight or both, were produced only in clear glass. Perche (1158) and Tête d'épervier (1139) came in clear, coloured and opalescent; and a number of models, including Tête de paon (1140), Grenouille (1146), Sanglier (1157), Vitesse (1160), Coq Houdan (1161), Coq nain and

101. Tête de bélier (1136): car mascot in polished glass, designed for illumination from below. (T8) 150mn

102. Tête d'épervier (1139):
polished opalescent glass. (T7)
61mm

Chrysis (1183), were made in clear and coloured glass. When the small opalescent Perche is lit it turns to an astonishing gold; a turquoise Tête de paon looks splendidly exotic, and Sanglier in a dark, dark grey, almost black, is particularly smart. Most exciting of all, perhaps, must have been (and could still be) a little watery green Grenouille disappearing into the night.

Each collector will have his own preferences, and it is difficult to give any hard and fast guidance as to prices. Victoire seems to have a special cachet and is probably the most sought after of all mascots; simply on account of its rarity, however, I would recommend the serious collector to look out for Coq Houdan. (The only examples of this model that I have ever seen were two miniature versions incorporated into the design of a hideous electric clock.) Other models that are particularly hard to track down include Vitesse (almost as expensive as Victoire), the medium-priced Faucon, Archer and Saint Christophe (1142), and the comparatively modest Lèvrier (1141).

7. Scent bottles and *garnitures de toilette*

'GIVE A WOMAN the best product you can compound,' wrote Lalique's famous friend and collaborator, François Coty, in 1906, 'present it in a perfect container (beautifully simple, but of impeccable taste), charge a reasonable price for it and a great business will arise such as the world has never seen.'

Unlike most such grandiose prophecies, this one rapidly came true. By so doing it largely determined the careers and fortunes of both men; it also profoundly affected the pockets, the appearance and the self-assurance of countless women of all ages and from all walks of life, for years to come.

Hitherto scent had only been available in hand-made bottles which were often more expensive to manufacture than their contents; the discovery by Lalique of a means of mass-producing such bottles so that they still carried an

103. OPPOSITE Bouchon fleurs de pommiers (493): clear glass bottle with satin finish and polished relief. (T2) 60mm

104. *Top left* Grey stained box with polished clear glass relief. (T2) 80mm; *Bottom left* Bouchon papillons (477): clear glass scent bottle with satin finish. (T2); *Right* Lunaria (482): clear glass scent bottle with a design of Honesty in dark grey staining. (T2) 90mm

105. Perles (601): cologne bottle, part of a dressing table set, in white glass with traces of blue staining. (T2) 120mm

106. Telline (508): white glass with satin finish and traces of blue staining. (T2) 100mm

aura of luxury and exclusiveness meant that midinettes in Paris or house-maids in London could, for the first time, own the same scents, in the same bottles, as their employers or mistresses. Dating and identification of these bottles present the collector with a number of problems, some of them insuperable. It was probably in 1906 that Coty commissioned his first bottles, and by the following year these were on display in Lalique's newly opened shop in the Place Vendôme; I have been unable to discover any reliable record of the designs of

107. Small commercial scent bottle made of clear glass and stained green. (T9) 70mm

these early bottles, and it seems likely that quite soon thereafter Coty was using them indiscriminately as containers for other scents. The names of the scents are readily ascertainable – Chypre, Violette de Coty, Effleurt, Muguet de Coty, Cyclamen, Ambre Antique, Styx, Jasmin de Corse all were available as scents before 1912, and several of them (e.g. Effleurt, Ambre Antique and Styx) were probably first marketed in bottles specially designed for them by Lalique. But by the early 1920s, and possibly well before, more than one scent was being sold in the same bottle; I have myself seen, at the Coty factory at Brentford, five different scents (Effleurt, Muguet des Bois, L'Aimant, Chypre and Emeraude) in one Lalique bottle bearing a motif of briars, and three others (Chypre, Paris and Styx)

108. *Left* Fleurs concaves (486): clear glass scent bottle with brown stained flowers moulded into the glass. (T2) 120mm; *Right* Cyclamen, a scent bottle designed for Coty, with a green stained design of nymphs. (T9) 130mm

in another bearing a motif of lizards. Other scent manufacturers for whom Lalique was to design and make bottles – e.g. Forvil, Houbigant, Nina Ricci, Roger et Gallet, Worth – may have been more consistent in this respect, but the only safe way of identifying a bottle by name is by reference either to the paper label which it may still carry, to the box in which it was sold, or to the moulded lettering that sometimes appears on the glass itself. Even if these problems do not arise, it is usually hard – if not impossible – to draw any certain conclusions as to the date of a bottle's manufacture, since many scents remained on the market for thirty or forty years.

Much safer for the collector, and probably more fun, is to concentrate on acquiring examples of the many different sizes in which Lalique manufactured certain designs, from minute sample *flacons* to massive 8oz Cologne bottles, such

109. OPPOSITE 'Je Reviens', a display scent bottle designed for Worth in clear glass with blue enamelling. (T6) Approximately 80mm

110. Dahlia, cologne bottle (615) and powder bowl (619) from a dressing table set; peach glass with satin finish and black enamelled stamens. (T1) 180mm, 140mm

111. Fleurettes (575): a pair of scent bottles in clear glass with edges stained blue. (T7) 160mm; Primevères (86): powder bowl in opalescent glass with traces of blue staining. (T6) 200mm

as those which he made for Worth's Je Reviens. Alternatively, the collector can endeavour to match up non-commercial bottles (i.e. those not specially designed to contain scent made by any one company) with the sets of co-ordinated containers which Lalique designed for the dressing table – for powder, or face cream or merely 'to put things in' – known as *garnitures de toilette*.

Lalique designed at least five different styles for these *garnitures*, each of them usually comprising *flacons* in four sizes, and *bôites* and bowls in two. The stylised Dahlia (615), revived by Marc Lalique after the second world war and still in production today, is usually in white glass but can also be found with a pink or green staining. Duncan (623) is a classical design from the twenties, its nude figures surrounded by a geometrical border; the attractive Perles (600), its pearls festooned in garlands, is most commonly found in frosted glass, often with the relief picked out in blue enamel. Epines (590), a set of squat bottles bearing

112. OPPOSITE ABOVE LEFT Advertisement for Worth in *L'Illustration*, December 1939

113. OPPOSITE ABOVE RIGHT 'Imprudence', a Worth scent bottle with silvered rims. (T9) 100mm

114. OPPOSITE BELOW Two commercial scent bottles. The stained bottle on the left was often produced with the rope design picked out in enamel. (T8, T5) 90mm, 85mm

Imprudence

Imprudence

WORTH
P A R I S

118. OPPOSITE White glass scent bottle with satin finish, hand stained with green. (T8) 120mm

115. LEFT Hélène (522): white glass with satin finish. (T2) 67mm

116. BELOW LEFT Hirondelles (503): satin finish with some trace of blue staining. (T2) 90mm

117. BELOW RIGHT Epines (593): white glass scent bottle with green stained background, part of a dressing table set. (T2) 96mm

119. *Top* Marguerites (69): polished clear glass bowl with brown staining. (T4) 85mm; *Below* Scent bottle in white glass with satin finish and polished relief. (T4) 60mm

Lalique's familiar thorn motif, is always accentuated in a variety of hand-stained finishes; so is Fleurettes (575), a set of plain glass bottles and bowls with a small geometrical border of flowers running down the square corners.

Sets of this kind had been in demand since at least the middle of the nineteenth century and throughout the Edwardian era, but they had usually been produced in expensive materials – silver, very often, or tortoise shell or cut-glass – and had largely been confined to the luxury market. Such materials (together with shagreen) were still in use during the twenties and thirties, but the comparatively inexpensive sets made by Lalique in mass-produced glass commanded an instant and continuing success.

8. Illuminated glass and light fittings

LIGHTING FORMED SO INTEGRAL A PART of Lalique's decorative and architectural techniques that if this book was intended as an academic study it would be sensible to consider the two together. However, from the collector's point of view it is necessary to preserve the distinction, if only for the obvious reason that many of Lalique's hanging lights and table lamps, in contrast to his panels and wall fittings, can still be discovered in shops and galleries. Even panels and wall fittings sometimes appear on the market, it is true – in 1974 I was lucky enough to find a panel identical to the ones above the lifts in Claridge's – but such occasions are rare. Collectors should examine any such items most carefully before identifying them as duplicates of Lalique's known work in other contexts; however similar such panels may appear on first sight, significant variations may often be detected both in size and in design.

120. Caravelle *surtout* presented by the city of Paris to the British King and Queen in 1938: it was identical to the model listed in the 1932 catalogue (1169)

LA VILLE DE PARIS A LEURS MAJESTES BRITANNIQUES
LE ROI GEORGE VI ET LA REINE ELIZABETH
20 JUILLET 1938

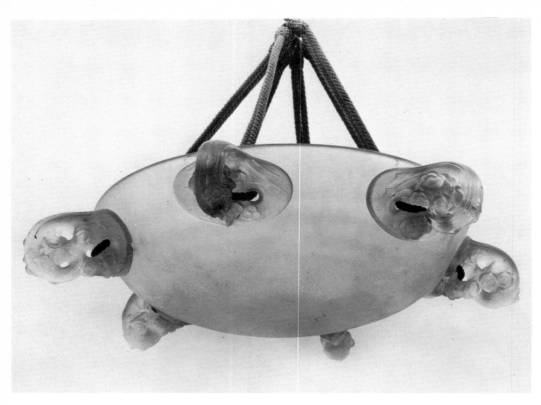

121. Ceiling light in white glass with satin finish and polished relief. (T5) 640mm

122. Detail of ceiling light reproduced in plate 120

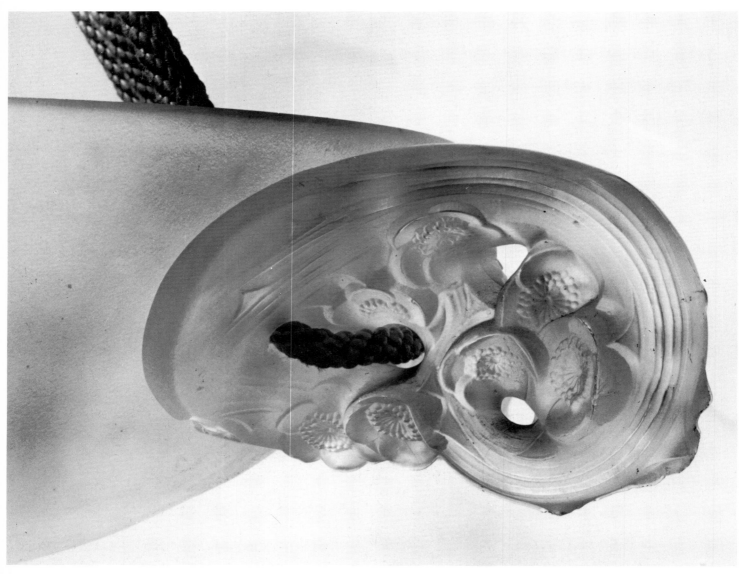

123. Acanthus: ceiling light in white glass with satin finish and polished relief. (T8) 440mm

In common with his contemporaries, Emile-Jacques Ruhlmann and Maurice Dufrène, Lalique did much to restore glass to the pre-eminent role in lighting lost when traditional chandeliers, using candles, went out of vogue in the second half of the nineteenth century. He had always been alive to the effect of electric light as a means of illuminating glass, and he had used it in glass panels for this purpose as early as 1902. By the beginning of the first world war he had started to combine moulded glass shades with wrought-iron bases, and by the end of the war he was hanging glass bowls from the ceiling, diffusing the light through the moulded surfaces of the glass and using the ceiling as a reflector. He exploited these techniques in order to create a two-tone effect; a relief of leaves or fruit, for instance, or clusters of mistletoe would act as a lens, concentrating the light into bright patches that contrasted with the surrounding soft glow. This fashionable device was a twentieth century innovation, and Lalique exploited it to great commercial effect.

Sometimes the motifs for these light bowls were co-ordinated with those of other unrelated objects: the Coquilles and Sirènes motifs, for instance, occur in tableware as well as in lighting. The lights would be suspended on specially designed chromium or bronze chains, or even on ropes, and they were frequently accompanied by matching wall fittings (appliques).

Another French glass company, Genet et Michon, is generally credited with the invention of moulded glass cornices to conceal electric bulbs, but it was Lalique who first had the flair and imagination to lay deliberate emphasis on the

124. Illustration from *La Sculpture Décorative Moderne* (Editions d'Art Charles Moreau, Paris)

Top Trois paons *surtout* (1110) 910mm; *Middle* Grande veilleuse table lamp; *Bottom* Deux cavaliers *surtout* (1109)

device and to use it as an important element in his interiors. Moulded in lengths of about 3ft and frequently decorated with a relief of fruit or flowers, they fitted together with great exactitude. The diffused light which they cast was described in a 1926 issue of *Commercial Art* as being 'of the utmost charm. Worth's shop at Cannes is lighted throughout in this way, and the result is most effective.'

Lalique used a similar device when he was commissioned to redecorate Maples in Tottenham Court Road, London. By setting the lights into the bronze cornicing which ran all the way round the central well of the store, he imparted strong horizontal detail to each floor level. He also used it in a domestic context, combining it with wall and centre lights and with rectangular glass troughs in the corridors leading away from the main rooms; these troughs would be decorated with motifs in high relief, in order to create a two-tone effect, and were supported in frames of chromium or bronze. Such lighting was considered to harmonise just as happily with the pale wood interiors, usually of sycamore or

125. *Left* Gros poisson, vagues (1100): white glass on bronze base. (T8) 300mm; *Right* Gros poisson, algues (1101): white glass on bronze base. (T8) 290mm

plane, which were the height of sophistication in the mid-twenties as it did with the art deco and modernist interiors, stark and arctic white, which came into fashion at the end of the decade.

Among the most monumental (and certainly the most useless) of all the illuminated objects which Lalique produced early in the thirties, were his massive *surtouts* – a series of heavy, crescent-shaped glass plaques, apparently designed for the centre of a dining table or sideboard. Nearly an inch thick and about 3ft long, they were mounted on bronze or wooden bases and moulded in deep intaglio. They bore a variety of illuminated designs; one of them, Oiseau de Feu (1111), is totally art nouveau in inspiration, and two others – Deux cavaliers (1109) and the beautiful Trois paons (1110) – are just as strongly Pre-Raphaelite. Most of the other designs, including the Caravelle (1169) which the City of Paris presented to King George VI and Queen Elizabeth in 1938, are frankly suburban; they serve to show Lalique's deliberate surrender to the commercialism of the thirties, and are a long way removed from the magnificent, slightly ominous fishes – Vagues (1100) facing right and Algues (1101) facing left – which reflect a far more vigorous spirit and a genuine feeling for the monstrous qualities of the deep.

By the beginning of the thirties fittings of this kind had become one of the most frequent clichés of contemporary interiors, private as well as public. They already extended well beyond Mayfair and the Faubourg St Honoré; they could be found in suburban homes in both capitals, not just in luxury apartment blocks like 60 Park Lane (where they still exist), and they were spreading rapidly into the provinces and beyond. Many of them were already illustrated in a catalogue, Lalique Lights and Decorations, issued by the Breves Galleries in 1928, on which I have relied for much of the information in this chapter.

In another catalogue, this one distributed in 1933 by Lalique's former agents, Edward Trower, the emphasis is largely on table lamps and hanging lights. Many of these are adapted (not always with notable success) from vases – Perruches (876), for instance.

When some of the larger vases were adapted by Lalique for this purpose an electric bulb would be placed inside the vase as well as under the shade, as an alternative or supplementary source of lighting. Lalique himself produced many lamps of this kind, but (in contrast to some of those shown in the Edward Trower catalogue) his were never drilled to accommodate the flex, which always came from the neck of the vase; the light fitting stayed in place either by balance or by means of a wooden bung. Formose (934) could be bought complete with a hardboard shade hand-painted to match the motif on the vase.

Among the most successful of Lalique's table lamps was a series (which features in his own 1932 catalogue) called Grande Veilleuse, resembling splendid, outsize scent bottles, and ranging in height from about 8in (Feuilles de Genet) to 17in (Inséparable). A magnificent example from this range, its thin glass crescent bursting out of the top of the opaline bottle and covered with a brilliant intaglio of blossom, is illustrated on page 106.

9. Glass in architecture

By the outbreak of the first world war many of the revolutionary ideas for the use of glass in the construction and decoration of buildings – ideas born while Lalique was still a young man – had started to bear fruit. The truth of a famous prophecy by Eugène Houtart – that glass was one of the two elements (the other was steel) which would characterise the twentieth century and give their name to it – was already evident.

Lalique never trained as an architect, but he was quick to grasp the opportunities which architecture offered him. The *âtelier* which he designed for himself in the Cours la Reine and completed in 1902 was the first serious statement of an interest which was to last all his life and to bring him many of his most remarkable commissions.

Built chiefly in a sober, rectilinear style, noticeably less exuberant than art nouveau, the house appears neatly to bridge the gap between the curvilinear

Maison Rouard

126. Display at Maison Rouard, a Paris gallery where Lalique frequently exhibited his glass

109

127. Iron gates designed by Bellery Desfontaines in 1913, incorporating two heavy glass medallions by Lalique

styles of that movement and the geometrical patterns that became fashionable in the twenties. Its façade rises over six storeys, the first three in dressed stone and the last three tiled and inset in imitation of the attics in some late medieval *château*; the stone pinnacles that flank the upper windows are like fossilized tree trunks, companions in spirit to turrets by Antonio Gaudi.

Apart from the wrought-iron balconies and a few panels of carved stonework, the emphasis of the façade falls chiefly on the front door. The branches of the two pine trees, set in high relief, their needles and cones laden with snow, converge from the two sides of the tall stone frame and spread onto the very glass of the door, creating a winter landscape of the kind which Lalique was to repeat many times during the next forty years. Its sophistication and sureness of touch contrast strongly with the uncertainties which haunt his other work at this period.

Ten years later, in 1912, Lalique made an exhibition salon entirely in glass for his friend François Coty to ship out to New York, and in the following year he collaborated with Bellery Desfontaines on the construction of a massive pair of wrought-iron entrance gates set with two large glass medallions pictured above, whose present whereabouts I have been unable to trace. In 1922 he constructed the dining room for the Exposition des Artistes Décorateurs described in Chapter 2; otherwise he seems not to have ventured much further into architecture until the 1925 Exhibition presented him with an opportunity once again to deploy his constructional skills, this time on a monumental scale.

Lalique mounted his own pavilion at the exhibition, and he designed others, equally impressive, for Sèvres and for Roger et Gallet. More spectacular than any of these, however, was the central obelisk which the organisers commissioned him to execute at the heart of the exhibition; this was the feature which symbolised the exhibition for Lalique's contemporaries throughout the world and has identified it for the historian ever since. The exhibition occupied the same magnificent site, including the Esplanade des Invalides and the Pont Alexandre III, as had its much larger predecessor, quarter of a century before. Every tree had to be preserved, and each pavilion was surrounded by gardens which had to be watered from the Seine. In order to dominate so vast a site, and to provide its focal point, Lalique chose to construct a glass fountain some 50ft high and consisting of seventeen octagonal tiers. On each tier of the obelisk, and at every corner, stood one of the 136 glass caryatids which were the archetypes for one of Lalique's most famous statuettes, Source de la Fontaine. Illuminated from within and from below, water cascading outwards and downwards from the topmost tier to the bottom, the fountain looked like a fantastic crystal pagoda – a magnificent assertion of Lalique's mastery of his medium and of the moment.

Other fountains were to follow – not only in Paris, at the Rond Point and

128. LEFT Photograph from Guillaume Janneau's book, *Modern Glass*, showing the Arcade des Champs Elysées; Lalique designed the fountain and glass lanterns

129. RIGHT Façade of the Worth shop in Cannes, executed in black marble and illuminated glass in 1926

inside the Arcade des Champs Elysées, but in Marseilles and even in London, at the Daily Mail Ideal Home Exhibition of 1931. All over France his chandeliers and wall lights could be found in hotels, shops and restaurants and even, by the beginning of the thirties, in churches. As his fame and his commissions spread, Lalique was not always able to exercise a tight control over the environment of his work, and sometimes his fittings were not treated as sympathetically as they deserved. There were lapses into a kind of 'Lalique kitsch' for which Lalique himself cannot be held responsible: the mirrored bathroom, for instance, designed by Oliver Hill for Gayfere House, the London home of Lady Mount Temple, in which Lalique birds were used as bath taps.

There were other architects, however, who genuinely understood Lalique's ideas and were capable of translating them into a truly sympathetic environment. Oswald Milne's setting of Lalique panels above Byron Inison's wrought-iron lift doors in Claridge's Hotel, London, was a happy inspiration; another was A. B. Grayson's design for the redecoration of St Matthew's Church at St Helier in Jersey. Commissioned in 1932 by Florence Lady Trent (previously Mrs Jesse Boot) in memory of her late husband, the interior of St Matthew's is as much a memorial to Lalique's genius as it is to Lord Trent's: it is dominated by a great glass cross flanked by glass pillars, all three in heavy relief and illuminated from within. In front of these is the altar and a glass-panelled communion rail, and on either side are two glass-screened chapels; all the windows carry a relief of Jersey and Madonna lilies, and the elegant, chalice-shaped font is striped alternately in clear and satin glass. A rather ordinary 1840s church has been transformed into a 1930s shrine.

This was not Lalique's first religious commission. Two years previously he had designed the interior fittings for a chapel in Normandy in similar style: the chromium-set altar rail was made of glass tiles, also bearing a motif of Madonna lilies, and the same design appeared on the crucifix and altar candlesticks, the reredos and in the apse window. This interior (the Chapelle de la Vierge Fidèle, near Caen) is described by Guillaume Janneau, author of the classic *Modern*

130. Panel, identical to those used by Oswald Milne in the redecoration of Claridge's in 1932

131. Reredos in the Lady Chapel of St Matthew's, St Helier, Jersey; illuminated glass with satin finish in a stainless steel frame. 1800mm

Glass (The Studio Limited, London, and William Edwin Rudge, New York, 1931), as 'one of the greatest successes, not only of the master himself, but of the whole of French decorative glass work.'

At the Salon d'Automne held in 1930 Lalique exhibited another chapel, also using Madonna lily tiles as his theme. The purity of this chapel's design, and the starkness of its architectural detail, served brilliantly to emphasise the beauty of the glass: dramatic and serene, it showed the perfection that could be achieved when Lalique was in total control of the context in which his work was to be displayed. The wrought-iron cases in which his jewelry was shown at the 1900

132. LEFT Glass font designed by Lalique for St Matthew's Church; satin and clear glass. Approximately 1000mm

133. OPPOSITE Detail of a window in St Matthew's

134. Detail of a pillar at the side of the main altar of St Matthew's

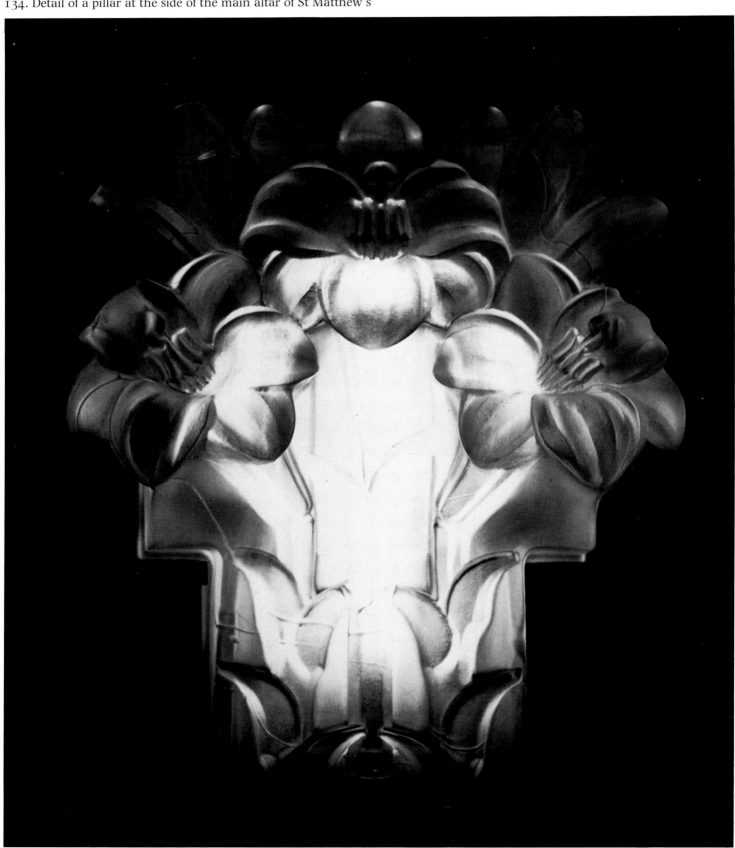

Exhibition achieved a similarly controlled effect, as did the marble dining-room of the Sèvres pavilion in 1925.

Perhaps the most spectacular of all Lalique's architectural assignments occurred in 1931, when he was commissioned to design the first-class dining-room for the *Normandie*, the most sophisticated passenger liner of that decade and probably of any other. Under the terms of the contract between her owners and the French government, the *Normandie* had to be 'not less than equal' to any other ship afloat or under construction, and she instantly acquired the status of ambassadress for all the luxury trades of France.

Situated in the centre of the ship, the dining-room was 305ft long, 46ft wide and 25ft high; at either end hung a colossal chandelier, and the entire length of the room was flanked by twelve free-standing monoliths of light, four-tiered and 23ft high. The walls were dressed in rough, unpolished glass and the coffered ceiling was inset with illuminated panels. The ship set out on her maiden voyage

135. Interior of the Côte d'Azur Pullman-car for which Lalique designed the partition panels

136. Artist's impression of the first-class dining room of the liner *Normandie*, launched in 1935 (from a special edition of *L'Illustration*, June 1932)

from Le Havre on 30th May 1935: for the first-class passengers that night dinner must have been a memorable occasion.

Lalique's work also featured strongly in other modes of public transport, notably rail. His first major commission for the Compagnie des Wagon-lits – a panel to decorate the sleeping car of the then French President, Alexandre Millerand – was executed in 1923. Six years later he designed and manufactured the statuettes which the company issued to commemorate the inauguration of its Côte d'Azur Pullman-car (illustrated on page 120), and he also made glass division panels and tableware for one of its carriages.

Two of the many shops for which Lalique supplied the decor deserve special mention, not only for themselves but as examples of the contrasting markets to which his work was considered appropriate. In London he provided Maples, suppliers of furniture to the rich bourgeoisie, with specially designed lighting for their enormous store in the Tottenham Court Road. And in Cannes Lalique designed the interior and exterior for the striking new shop opened by Worth, the great French costumier. Its façade was clad in plain black marble, inset with a huge illuminated 'Worth' in glass lettering almost 2ft high; the giant architrave was constructed in seven bands of moulded glass, lit from within and stepping sharply inwards towards the plain glass door. It was a brilliantly original concept, no less brilliantly executed.

137. Door handle, in the form of a bee, with satin finish and polished relief. (T4) 60mm

10. Small objects

Statuettes, ink-wells and blotters, clocks,
mirrors, glass jewelry, boxes and
sweetdishes

FOR THE COLLECTOR, the appeal of the many smaller items manufactured by Lalique, sometimes in huge quantities, is obvious. Some of them are widely available, a few can still be purchased quite cheaply and, of course, most of them require very little space to display. It is for these reasons that I have grouped so many disparate types of object into this one chapter; if it encourages the collector to specialize in one particular area it will have served a useful purpose.

Statuettes

The heavily stylized female figure, usually intended to convey robust health as well as beauty, is one of the decorative clichés of the thirties, as familiar on posters and bathing costumes as it was on calendars and every kind of packaging. It was natural that Lalique should adapt it to the mantlepiece, and his 1932 catalogue lists fourteen different models of statuette, one of them made in thirteen sizes. Lalique's unique contribution to this stereotype lay in the zest with which he carried out his designs, and the technical ingenuity with which he executed them.

140. OPPOSITE Naïade (832): opalescent glass with satin finish and polished relief. (T2) 130mm

138. LEFT Statuette issued by the Compagnie des Wagon-lits to commemorate the inauguration of the Côte d'Azur Pullman-car in 1929

139. RIGHT Amour assis (3): white glass box with satin finish and traces of blue staining. (T8) 140mm

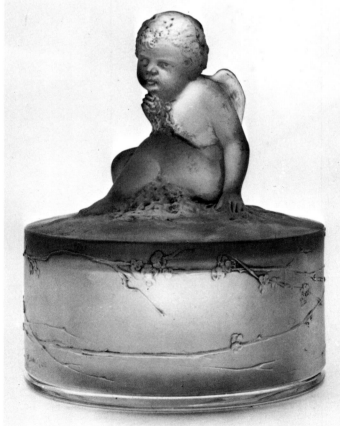

Two of Lalique's most popular statuettes, Joueuse de flûte (826) and Tête penchée (827), are a notable cross between conventional statues and plaques in high relief: the detail on each is extremely clear and intricate, the hair appears to float backwards, every flower in the surrounding garlands is distinct – yet neither of them looks or feels in the least fragile. Voilée, mains jointes (828), unprotected by any plaque, appears stark and vulnerable by contrast, while the compact design of Sirène (831) and Naïade (832) emphasizes their static, frozen quality. Suzanne (833), usually known as Suzanne au bain, and Thaïs (834) display Lalique's capacity for interpreting the spirit of art deco at its most sophisticated and delicate: in each case the gossamer fabric draped over the

141. OPPOSITE Sirène (831): opalescent glass with satin finish and polished base. (T2 and T8) 100mm

142. Naïade (221): white glass with satin design in intaglio. (T4) 100mm

extended arms of the central figure acts as a subtle support, and at the same time lends it a magical transparent quality when lit from below. A metal base incorporating a light for this purpose, was an optional extra on both these models. Grande nue, bras levés (835 and 836) is more conventional in style, harking back to art nouveau rather than to art deco, while Source de la fontaine (837–849) is a spectacular evocation, both in origin and in style, of the 1925 Paris Exhibition (see Chapter 9).

144. OPPOSITE LEFT Nue (836): white glass with satin finish, on wooden base. (T3) 400mm

145. OPPOSITE RIGHT Moyenne nue (830): white glass with satin finish. (T2) 150mm

Ink-wells and blotters

Throughout his working life, both as jeweller and as glass-maker, Lalique designed countless objects for the desk – paper-weights, ashtrays, pin trays, photograph frames, lamps and, more specifically, blotters and ink-wells. Over a dozen of the latter are listed in the 1932 catalogue, ranging in price from 75 francs for Nénuphar (425) to 1,800 francs for the rectangular Colbert (438), produced in a limited edition of fifty. The plain geometrical design of Sully (439) provides an interesting contrast with 4 Sirènes (434), a circular ink-well with sea nymphs swirling around it. Lalique also devised an imaginative range of eight hand-blotters (150–157), each with a different motif on its glass handle; like his seals, they were both useful and luxurious, and they sold extremely well.

143. Mûres (156): white glass blotter with satin finish and polished relief. (T3) 160mm

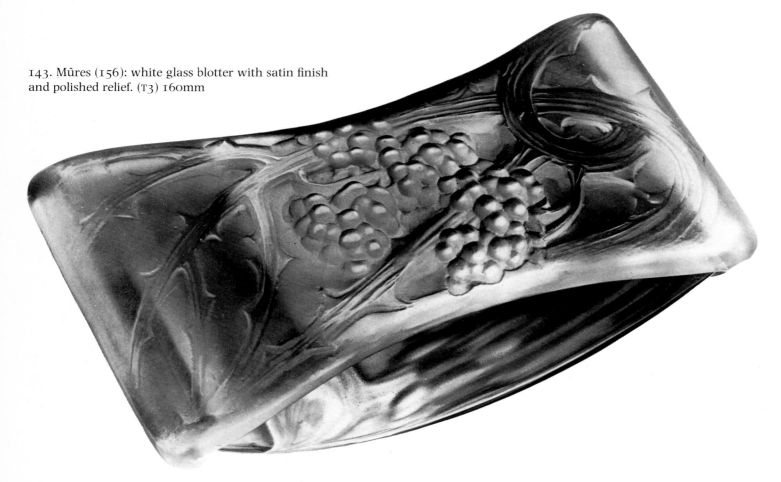

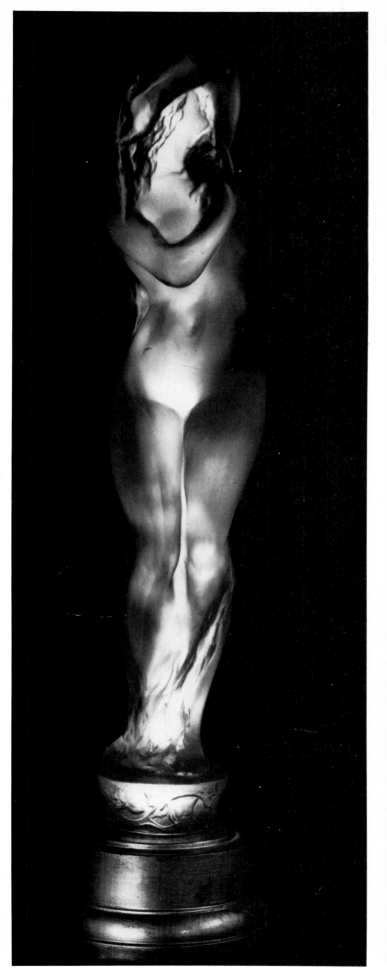

Clocks

The 1932 catalogue lists nineteen different designs of clock – eleven of them as *pendules* (ranging from 8in to 14in wide), the remainder as *pendulettes* (about 6in). Five of the *pendules* were electric and cost between 950 and 3,500 francs; all the others had eight-day movements, the *pendules* costing between 1,000 and 1,175 francs and the *pendulettes* between 500 and 850. Of the electric clocks Le Jour et la Nuit (728) is particularly fine; its 14in round disc of blue or smokey glass depicts a naked woman in relief on one side of the 4in wide dial, the relief making her appear much darker than the naked male in intaglio on the other.

The *pendulettes* were much the more popular of the two ranges. Some of them – e.g. Inséparables (765) – were also used as photograph frames, and as clocks were supplied with a variety of movements. Naïades (764), for instance, could be purchased either with a plain gilt metal face, or with a white enamel face with

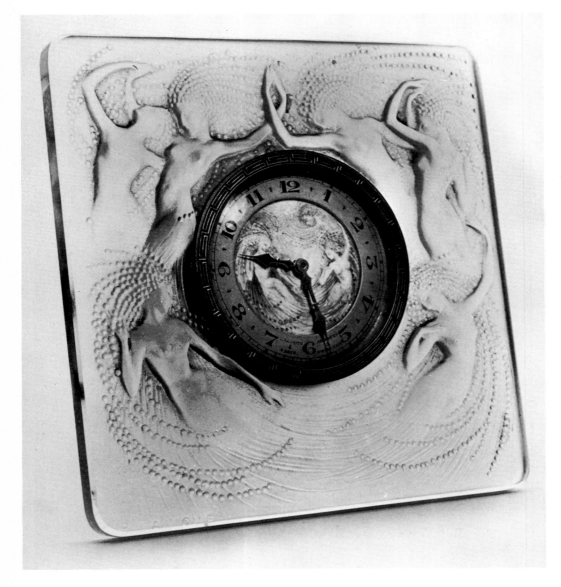

146. Naïades (764): clock in opalescent glass with satin finish; the face is hand-painted ivory. (T8) 110mm

147. Inséparables (765): clock in opalescent glass with satin finish. (T8) 110mm

black numerals, or with an ivory face hand-painted to match the design on the glass frame (see page 126). Collectors intending to purchase a clock should be especially careful to ensure that the movement is either in good repair or, if not, that it can be repaired at a reasonable price.

Mirrors

Two kinds of mirror figure in the 1932 catalogue – small hand mirrors that lie flat on the dressing table, and a pair of larger round standing mirrors held in mahogany frames. The hand mirrors are deliberately timeless in design – their simplicity is modern, but they also have a patina and styling reminiscent of the ancient world. Some of them, like Narcisse couché (675), bore long glass handles, others were designed to lie face downwards on the dressing table in order to display their decorated backs: 2 oiseaux (677) has a simple glass grip

148. Acanthes (3460): jardinière in white glass with satin finish and traces of blue staining

149. Seal with satin finish and grey hand-staining. (T8) 70mm

150. ABOVE Deux oiseaux (677): back of a hand-mirror in white glass with satin finish and lightly polished relief. (T7) 160mm

incorporated into the design across the back, while Muguets (684) and 3 paons (679) were designed to be held by an opulent-looking silk tassle. In 1924 Lalique made a long-handled hand mirror, similar in style to Narcisse, for Princess Victoria of Baden, wife of the King of Sweden; its silvered glass back was elaborately decorated with a relief of swallows and briars and was probably cast in *cire perdue*.

151. 'Replique' scent bottle in gilt metal and satin glass, worn as a pendant. Enamelled signature. 50mm

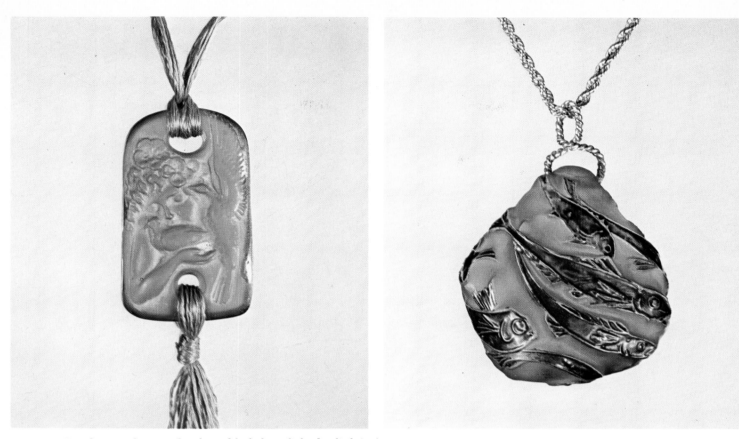

152. LEFT Pendant with satin finish and lightly polished relief. (T4) 40mm

153. RIGHT Pendant with a frosted glass surface, giving the appearance of rock crystal; the fishes are in blue enamel. (T5) 50mm

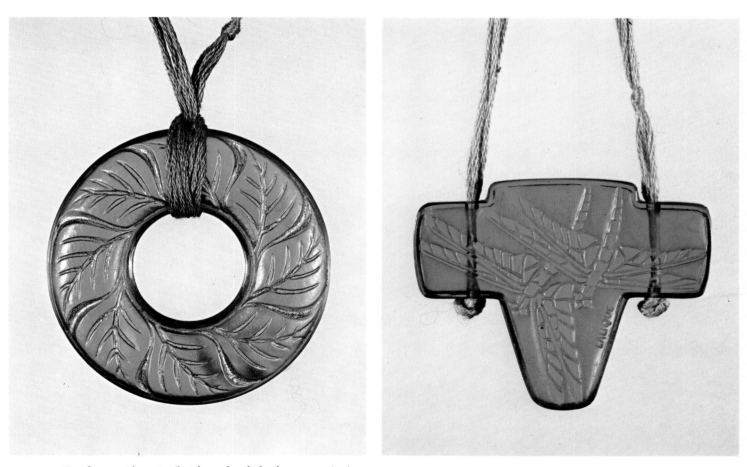

154. LEFT Pendant with satin finish and polished reverse. (T4) 50mm

155. RIGHT Pendant with satin finish and polished relief. (T4) 40mm

Glass jewelry

Lalique was selling glass bracelets, necklaces and pendants as early as 1921 and it is probable that most of those designs were still listed in the 1932 catalogue. None of these items, however, bear any relation to the far more expensive jewelry which Lalique was producing before the first world war: even the most expensive necklace listed in 1932, Boules (1513), cost only 1,050 francs, none of the nineteen bracelets cost more than 600 francs, and the average price of the fifteen pendants was 175 francs. All these items were executed in moulded glass and held together with silk or elastic cord; vibrant and glittering, they often looked more like confectionery than jewelry, and although they were

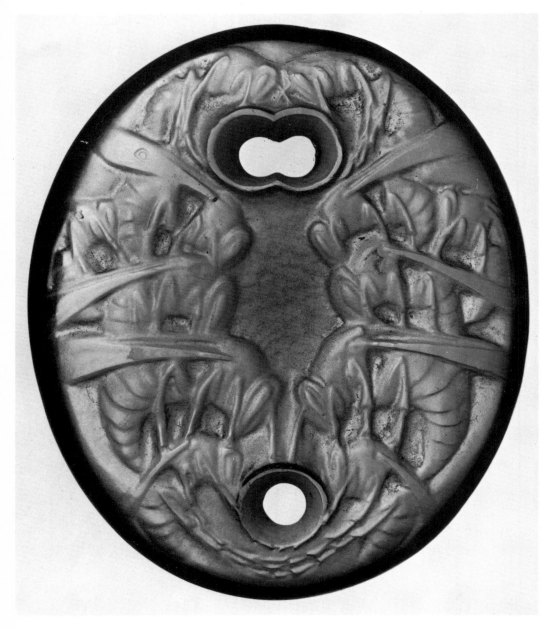

156. LEFT Pendant in blue glass with satin finish depicting wasps. (T4) 55mm

157. ABOVE Pendant in opalescent glass, with design of lilies of the valley. (T8) 60mm

158. OPPOSITE Pendant in opalescent glass, with design of lilies. (T8) 55mm

159. Blue glass pendant with satin surface and lightly polished relief. (T4) 40mm

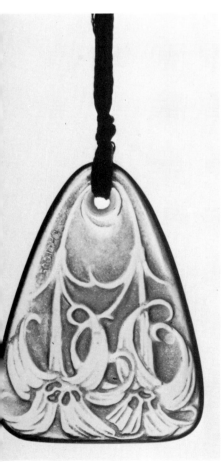

surprisingly resilient they were usually regarded as expendable; glass pendants and rings would naturally not be treated with the same respect by their owners as would their more precious counterparts, and there can have been little incentive to re-string the glass beads of a broken necklace or bracelet, however pretty. Plain glass discs with an intaglio design of nymphs and garlands were frequently sold as brooches, with their backs silvered to impart a more jewel-like quality; in addition to the pretty butterflies and dragon-flies which one would expect in such a range there were also a number of rather alarming devils and the faces of dogs baring huge, fang-like teeth.

160. Dinard (78): white glass box
with satin finish. (T1) 110mm

161. Cyprins (42): box in
opalescent glass. (T8) 255mm

Boxes and sweet-dishes

Apart from the sheer quantity of Lalique's boxes and sweet-dishes – over eighty different models are listed in the 1932 catalogue – the range of prices quoted indicates the immense variety in their style and elaboration. While the average price listed for a white glass box was about 200 francs, one of them – the six-sided Saint-Nectaire (76) – cost a mere 40 francs; there were about a dozen at between 60 and 100 francs, and the two cigar boxes listed – Roméo (79), almost as heavy as a butter dish, and the leafy Corona (80) – cost 550 and 600 francs respectively. Such a vast range of styles can form a particularly rewarding basis for the collector whose space and budget are limited; and any such collection could well be extended to include the powder boxes with glass tops and card bases which Lalique made for cosmetic firms such as Houbigant and D'Orsay, as well as their glass pots and jars.

162. Black glass box with patinated design on the lid in the form of a chrysanthemum. (T4) 85mm

163. Roger (75): box in white
glass with black enamel relief.
(T1) 130mm

164. Box in frosted green glass
with polished relief and silver
scarab hinges and clasp. (T8)
717mm

IT IS ONE OF THE SADDER IRONIES of collecting Lalique glass that the chances of ever seeing, let alone acquiring, any of the objects into which the artist concentrated the essence of his genius are so remote as to be almost negligible. Throughout his working life – from his earliest days as an apprentice jeweller until, by the middle of the thirties, his hands had become crippled with arthritis – Lalique adopted the *cire perdue* method of moulding (see Chapter 12) in order to express his strongest creative impulse. The glass which he produced by this means is as visibly different from his commercially moulded output as is an original Picasso from any reproduction, however well executed; and, alas, it is just about as rare. The result is that, for the collector, its interest is almost entirely academic: it is virtually impossible to purchase such objects, other than in auction rooms or galleries where their market value has already been accurately assessed, and it is even more difficult to study any number of them together.

165. *Cire perdue* study of two sinister animals. Lalique has used his fingerprints to create the texture of the light grey surface

Perhaps the single most distinctive feature of *cire perdue*, apart from the absence of a moulding mark, lies in its texture. Other than at the rim or base Lalique seldom polished such objects; the sides and all the main surfaces were left in their natural state, sculptured but not 'finished', dull and even lifeless to look at, rough and almost crunchy to feel. The artist's finger-prints, intended as a sort of signature, have become part of the matt surface; you have only to look at the object to recognize that it is lighter and more fragile than any of its manufactured counterparts, and far more personal to the artist.

Since by its very nature *cire perdue* ensures that anything so produced is a unique object, unrepeated and unrepeatable, the people for whom Lalique executed such commissions were more commonly his own friends and colleagues. He made a *cire perdue* clock for the Queen of Egypt and a silver-backed hand mirror for the Queen of Sweden; he executed a fine bronze *cire*

166. OPPOSITE *Cire perdue* vase with a design of eucalptus leaves in opaque, rough textured glass. 6omm

167. *Cire perdue* vase in opaque, rough textured glass with hazel-nut and leaf motifs. 6omm

perdue portrait of his wife; and for his friend Ferdinand Khnopff, the Belgian symbolist painter and art critic, he made a *cire perdue* bronze of a pet tortoise which died after Khnopff had banished it out of doors for making too much noise in his studio. I have in my own possession a rather nasty little bibelot, made in *cire perdue* glass and bearing Lalique's own finger-prints; two tiny animals, with the bodies and tails of mice, the teeth of rats and the ears of rabbits, crouched on one side of a small bowl, ready and anxious to pounce. Small as it is, the object possesses several of the qualities that distinguish Lalique's *cire perdue* from his commercial output: the glass is stippled, it bears Lalique's own finger-prints, and the individual features of the animals which it depicts, however improbable their combination, are entirely 'realistic' in themselves. There is no pandering to the sentimental tastes of the mass market, no sign of the deliberate 'prettiness' which marks so much of Lalique's commercial output: instead, the tiny animals convey the same strange and haunted feeling which the artist occasionally imparted to far larger beasts, such as the two Gros Poissons (described in Chapter 8) which Lalique manufactured on a commercial basis. Many of his *cire perdue* animals in glass, like most of those in his jewellery, bear something of this nightmare quality: in the Toledo Museum, for instance, there is a squat, bowl-shaped vase resting on a heavy ebony plinth, its clear glass obscured by the evil masks of four predatory fish. The effect is macabre and frightening – but it is also typical of Lalique's artistry at its most brilliant and undiluted.

12. Techniques

LALIQUE'S FOREMOST CLAIM to fame is that of an artist. That claim, however, rests to an unusual degree on his technical proficiency, and no appreciation of his work can be complete without some attempt to understand the techniques, many of them acquired while he was a jeweller, which Lalique either adapted or invented during his thirty years as a manufacturer of glass. It is clear that by 1907, when Lalique first began to work for François Coty, he already understood the material properties of glass, and its response to mechanical processes, far better than

168. Degas (66): box in white glass with satin finish. (T8) 75mm

170. Magnificent *cire perdue* bowl in opaque, rough textured white glass with four grotesque fish masques. Approximately 200mm

many of his contemporaries who had used the medium for years. Lalique always experimented, and he learnt from his experiments while others remained blinkered.

To appreciate the scale of Lalique's technical achievement, it is worth recalling that the manufacture of pressed or moulded glass only began on a commercial scale at the start of the nineteenth century, and then only in order to produce cheap imitations of expensively hand-worked glass; the mechanical processes applied by Lalique, first to scent bottles and later to luxury glass of almost every kind, had hitherto been confined almost entirely to bottles for medicine and beer and to a few poor reproductions of cut-glass decanters. What Lalique and Coty conceived between them was just as significant a leap forward in technology as it was in terms of commercial practice. The secret of mass-producing scent bottles lay chiefly in the substances of the glass. Lalique's discovery of 'demi-crystal' – or rather his re-discovery of its properties – meant that the elaborate and numerous designs required by Coty could be fashioned on a mass scale. This highly ductile material, containing less than 30 per cent lead oxide in its composition, was not affected by the temperature, however high and however constant; and unlike 'pure' crystal, which required lengthy cutting and polishing, it needed very little finishing after it came out of the mould.

The four methods used by Lalique for the casting of his glass need to be clearly differentiated. They were as follows:

1. *Cire perdue*

An original wax model was covered in plaster and left to dry. It was then warmed and the melted wax allowed to run out, leaving a mould into which molten glass could either be poured (in the case of a small figure, for instance) or blown in order to form a vase, perhaps, or a flask. The plaster had to be removed

169. Vase gobelet, 6 figurines (903): the figures are in heavy relief with a satin finish and traces of blue staining

after the glass had cooled, thus destroying the mould and leaving a unique piece of glass which might itself be worked on in order to become the prototype for a new design.

Cire perdue was an ancient form of casting which Lalique had previously employed in order to fashion precious metals, either for the finely chiselled or enamelled backgrounds which featured in much of his jewelry or for the heads or bodies of the mythological creatures which formed some of its central motifs. He used it also for casting table centre-pieces in silver, for metal adornments to his glass and alabaster chalices and for a massive bronze peacock which he sculpted in 1898–9.

2. *Refractory moulded glass*

During his experiments with making glass panels for his house in Cours la Reine, Lalique re-discovered a technique for making glass-paste which had been lost for centuries. He would first make a clay refractory mould by taking an impression from a model, usually made in wax; he would then fill the mould with cullet (crushed and broken glass) and place it in a furnace, and at the correct temperature the cullet would melt into a paste which found its own level within the mould. When the glass cooled its contraction would cause the mould to collapse, without damaging the contents, and a new clay mould could be made from the original, for use in the next firing.

3. *Pressed glass*

A plunger, worked either manually or mechanically, would force molten glass evenly around an open metal mould, which was opened after the glass was sufficiently cool for annealing to commence. The intense pressure generated by this process would ensure bold and forceful definition.

Annealing is the process whereby stresses are removed from molten or heated glass: the cooled object is slowly brought back to a very high temperature, thus relaxing the glass. Lalique's knowledge of this process is particularly impressive: a vase like Tourbillons (see page 38), with its dramatic contrasts in thickness, would require infinite care, and even small objects, such as the Coq nain mascot, could take twenty-four hours to anneal. A thick glass statuette might take three months to cool down after annealing, and temperatures would need to be most carefully controlled throughout this period.

4. *Blown glass*

A 'gather' of molten glass would be taken from a crucible or small vat and blown into a closed metal mould. This mould would then open into four segments, like an orange, in order to release the finished article.

Some coloured vases produced by this method appear to contain separate layers of colour. This was achieved by allowing the original 'gather', having cooled for a few seconds, to be covered by a new 'gather' of another colour before it was blown into the mould. Judgement and timing were critical – the whole operation might take only thirty seconds.

Wine glasses required a combination of both the latter processes, achieved on a

171. Saint-Denis (388): fine example of a goblet created by combining hand-blown and power-press techniques. The stem is partly enamelled. (TI) 170mm

single machine. The stem was formed first, in a power press; after the plunger had been removed the metal mould for the bowl was swung over the top into a position which would permit the bowl to be blown directly onto the stem. The moulded foot was applied later. When plain decanters were being blown the glass blower would revolve the glass in the mould in order to remove all trace of the joints when it was removed. In the final stages, when the moulded stopper was being ground to fit the decanter, both items were numbered in case they became separated at a later date.

Most of Lalique's moulded glass required the minimum of finishing. The tops

GLASSWARE—CONTINENTAL

VASE OF PRESSED GLASS WITH SILVERED BRONZE
BASE BY P. GENET AND L. MICHON, PARIS
(see also page 96)

VASE OF ENGRAVED GLASS BY RENÉ LALIQUE, PARIS

TABLE OF ENGRAVED GLASS BY RENÉ LALIQUE, PARIS
(see also page 163)
(Photo Rep.)

172. Page from a 1927 issue of
The Studio. The vase (top right) is
Grimpereaux (987)

and bases of blown pieces might need to be cut and polished, and the mould marks on pressed pieces might require smoothing; additional decorative work was no more than an occasional luxury. Certain large hand-blown objects required further processing, however, usually because the glass had cooled too rapidly to permit the relief to form in sufficient detail: as much as 1mm of glass might have to be polished off a large hand-blown vase like Gros scarabées (892), using rouge and high-speed buffers for the purpose. The moulds for smaller blown vases could be heated from the outside by gas torches, thus keeping the glass hot for long enough to ensure perfect conformation with the mould. It was important, however, to ensure that the glass and metal did not reach the same temperature at the same time, as otherwise they would stick together.

The frosted effect characteristic of much of Lalique's glass – sometimes spread over the complete surface, sometimes only on details – was achieved by the application of an acid; this effect could be softened by polishing the high relief of the design, and some Lalique objects also have an additional patina, created by exposing the acided glass to a mixture of gases, which gives them the illusion of antiquity. Lalique used this technique to particularly good effect in glass brooches, pendants, paper-weights and medallions.

Enamelling, another of Lalique's most successful forms of decoration, was usually achieved by combining powdered enamel with a binder and painting the mixture onto the glass, prior to firing. Lalique was equally adept, however, at creating a stained effect by a more subtle means of enamelling which required two firings; this resulted in a soft, almost watery appearance, less durable than the bold lines of shiny colour obtained by the first method, but it was equally if not more attractive. The staining on such pieces is delicate, and they should only be washed in warm water and soap.

I am indebted to Mr Martin Hunt of the Royal College of Art for the following notes on additional chemicals melted into the glass mix in order to produce Lalique's most characteristic colours:

RED	*gold chloride, selenium or cadmium oxide or copper oxide; nickel in lead glass.*
GREEN	*nickel and chrome oxide.*
VIOLET	*nickel and manganese oxides.*
PURPLE	*manganese dioxide (in high concentrations this produces a deep purplish brown); nickel in high alkaline glass containing potash.*
BLUE	*cobalt oxide; nickel in soda glass.*
TURQUOISE	*copper.*
YELLOW	*oxides of iron, silver chloride or cadmium sulphide; basic sulphur in non-lead glasses.*
OPAL	*produced either by imperfect mixtures of phosphates etc., or by crystallization when the glass contains fluorides.*
AMBER	*manganese dioxide and iron dioxide.*
BLACK	*cobalt dioxide and manganese dioxide.*

13. Trademarks

EVERY ITEM manufactured by the Lalique factories, other than some of those specially commissioned for other firms (such as certain types of scent bottle), bore Lalique's trademark in one form or another. The collector will soon learn to recognize the eleven variations illustrated below, and it is possible that he will discover others – either as the result of human error in the execution of those applied by hand or because there may be marks which have not yet come to my attention. The first five and the last are etched into the glass, the remainder are moulded.

T1. Block lettering achieved by using a stencil and sand-blasting the glass, leaving a frosted impression. This mark is usually associated with objects produced from a power press – mostly vases, tableware, and a few paper-weights and mascots; it is still used by the Cristal Lalique company, without the initial R.

R. L. ALIQUE
FRANCE

T2. This script facsimile of René Lalique's signature, with or without the addition of the word 'France'* and the design number, was normally reserved for hand-blown objects. It was also occasionally added when the moulded trademark on an object produced from a power press was insufficiently clear.

R. Lalique France N° 3152

T3. Etched with a small wheel and found only on objects produced by power press in the early thirties.

R **LALIQUE**
FRANCE

T4. Usually associated with small-scale objects, this etched mark looks as though it has been scratched on to the surface of the glass. The initial R was omitted from a few objects produced before the second world war, and the mark is used in this form by Cristal Lalique today.

R. Lalique

* The addition of the word 'France' to any of the trademarks probably indicates that the object was produced in or after 1926, the year Britain first insisted on the naming of the country of origin on all imported goods.

R LALIQUE

T5. Finely engraved, this mark is etched on objects produced by power press prior to 1930.

T6. Bad definition (as drawn) indicates that the object was hand-blown, since the rapidly cooling glass could not be injected with sufficient force around the raised relief to obtain a perfect moulding. If the definition is good, the object was probably produced on a power press.

LALIQUE

T7. Produced in the same manner as T6, but not so common; may be found, for instance, on the Fleurettes (575) dressing table set and the 2 oiseaux (677) hand mirror.

R. LALIQUE   FRANCE.

T8. Except for a few hand-blown decanters*, this mark was reserved for objects produced by power press, and definition is therefore usually good. It is found on statuettes, mascots, paper-weights and light fittings. Occasionally it appears without the initial R.

T9. Whereas most trademarks were placed off-centre, this one is usually to be found in the middle of bowls, where it blends in with the design. Note the double-tailed Q.

T10. Associated with objects produced by power press and usually found moulded along the rim or outside edge.

R Lalique
France

T11. Like T4, this circular mark looks as though it has been scratched onto the surface. It is associated only with a few wine glasses.

* These were hand-blown into a mould; because their all-round design was not revolved, and because the thinner glass stayed hot for a longer time, a better impression was achieved than was possible by means of method 6.

14. Design numbers

THE ILLUSTRATED CATALOGUE which the Lalique factory issued in 1932 provides a fascinating insight into the commercial tastes and predilections for which Lalique had by then learnt to cater. It would be difficult to imagine a more precise reflection of the manner in which a fashionable consumer industry obeys the laws of supply and demand at a given moment, and for that alone the catalogue's value is considerable. It is not for this reason, however, that I have chosen to devote so much space to it.

The catalogue was massive: it ran to over one hundred pages, each measuring about 9½in (24cm) deep by 12in (30cm) wide, and almost every one of the 1,500 or so items which it listed was separately illustrated. A typical entry in the text reads as follows:

Numéro	Planche		Blanc	Couleur
801	75	PRESSE-PAPIERS 2 aigles	250	300

Numéro indicates the design number; *planche* (plate, in the sense of picture) is a cross-reference to the page on which the object was illustrated; and the figures under *blanc* and *couleur** indicate the item's retail price in French francs, respectively in clear glass (with or without a patina) and in coloured glass (opalescent, blue, green, brown etc., according to one of the Conditions of Sale listed at the front of the catalogue).

Lalique for Collectors by Katharine Morrison McClinton – the only book, so far as I know, that identifies a substantial quantity of Lalique's design numbers – states that the figures under *blanc* and/or *couleur* indicate the quantities of that item held in stock when the catalogue was published. This cannot be so: one of the Conditions of Sale which preface the catalogue refers specifically to *les prix qui figurent au présent catalogue* (the prices quoted in this catalogue); four other references to prices occur in the other twelve conditions, and none at all to quantities; and a footnote on page 16 of the catalogue states that certain models of paper-weight *peuvent être montés en bouchons de radiateur moyennant un supplément de 135 frs* (may be mounted as a car mascot for an additional payment of 135 francs). In addition, the consistency of the margin by which the figures listed under *couleur* or *émail* exceeds those under *blanc* points conclusively, in my opinion, to the fact that these figures indicate price, not quantity.

The catalogue's purpose was to inform wholesale traders of the prices charged at Lalique's shop in the Place Vendôme, and to warn them that no item should be sold for less – *pour quelque raison et de quelque façon que ce soit* (for whatever reason and in whatever manner). Such prices carry little significance today, however, and I have not thought it necessary to include them in the list which follows. They merely serve as poignant reminders of the period when a clear

* In the lists of dressing table sets and scent sprays, *émail*; in the lists of jugs, decanters, goblets and glasses, *couleur ou émail*.

glass Saint Christophe car mascot (1142) could be bought for 285 francs (about £3 or $11 in 1932) and even a coloured Coq Houdan (1161), now one of the rarest of all mascots, for a mere 400 francs. The lovely opalescent Joueuse de flûte (826) cost 1,500 francs (almost £16 or $58) – a steep price, even then, for a statuette; but the most expensive of all the vases listed, Grande Boule, lierre (877), could be bought in clear glass for only 2,000 francs and is now a museum piece. It is also interesting to note that the difference in retail price between the clear and coloured versions was seldom more than ten or fifteen per cent – an indication, perhaps, that marketing considerations played a more significant role in determining Lalique's price structure than did the cost of manufacture.

Whatever value the modern collector may attach to such information, this listing of two distinct prices provides him with his only wholly reliable evidence as to whether a particular item was manufactured at that time in more than one type of glass; and the additional fact that more than one design number was sometimes allocated to one particular subject – e.g. the thirteen numbers allocated to Source de la fontaine statuettes (837 to 849) – proves the existence of corresponding variations either in the size or the form of its presentation.

Since the names which Lalique adopted for many of his objects were listed in a form of shorthand, and many of these names are either repeated or resemble each other very closely, I have thought it better to retain them in the original French and to append a glossary (page 178). For ease of reference I have re-listed the entries according to the exact numerical order of their design numbers (in the catalogue they were grouped, rather loosely, into categories corresponding to their intended use and were frequently repeated); but I have retained Lalique's own headings wherever practicable, and as a further aid to identification I have appended my own alphabetical list of categories (page 177), showing the relevant design numbers for each.

It is, of course, to the design numbers that the collector will wish to refer most frequently, either to identify an item which he has already found or to ear-mark one which he hopes to find in the future. It is therefore important to understand the principles which Lalique seems to have adopted in assigning these numbers, and also to realize that some of these principles were applied so arbitrarily that any conclusions based on them must always be of a tentative nature*. The first and most obvious problem arises in relation to the frequent gaps in the numerical sequence. These may be very short – sometimes consisting only of one or two numbers: 983 is obviously a vase, for instance, just as 1506 to 1508 are clearly necklaces; but in several areas (e.g. 527 to 574 and 1203 to 1326) the gaps are much wider, and the huge jump at the end (from 3768 to 5244) calls for some explanation.

There are a number of possible explanations for the longer gaps. Some of them may represent the firm's deliberate policy, allowing for the possibility of later extensions to a particular range of objects; others may be accounted for by the

* Design numbers should not be confused with the individual numbers – usually of up to five digits broken into two groups (e.g. 146-25 or 9-31) – which Lalique sometimes engraved on his own *cire perdue* objects before they were cast. The second group of these digits probably refers to the year in which the object was executed, the first to the order of execution.

fact that certain items were no longer in production in 1932, or were temporarily out of stock; a few omissions were probably accidental; and the final 1,500 numbers may have been allocated to light fittings and architectural glass, none of which figure in this catalogue. In those instances where I believe there to be a real possibility of identifying the missing designs I have merely listed the number by itself, to enable the collector to fill in the missing details. In a few instances (979, 996, 5127–5130) I have been able to do this myself, naturally without attributing a name to the object or specifying whether it was manufactured in other kinds of glass.

Dating of individual items presents the collector with another set of problems – problems on which the 1932 catalogue sheds some light, but not much. 3751 (Verre à pied, 4 grenouilles) was illustrated in Gustave Geffroy's monograph (see Chapter 2) published in 1922, the year that Lalique opened his new factory in Alsace. If, therefore, one were to assume – a reasonable assumption, one might think – that the design numbers followed a chronological sequence, it would seem obvious that all objects bearing an earlier number were already in production by that date; and there is other evidence, of a documentary as well as an aesthetic nature, which would support such a theory. However, the existence of the long gaps which I have already discussed means that it cannot be safe to rely on such an assumption; only, therefore, when I have seen documentary proof that an object was already in existence in a certain year have I indicated that fact in the English notes, after the description of the object. Such an entry does not, of course, establish the date of the object's original manufacture, which may have been much earlier. The collector should also recall that Lalique continued to produce new designs for some six years after publication of the 1932 catalogue – e.g. the chaffinch bowl.

There is a further point which the collector should bear in mind. Not only does Lalique appear sometimes to have been quite arbitrary in selecting the sequence of his design numbers; he seems also to have followed different, and even conflicting principles in deciding whether physically to apply the chosen number to the object. I have frequently come across two identical items, of which one carried a design number and the other did not; its absence, however disappointing to the collector, need not discredit any attribution of the object, nor should it diminish the item's market value. The serious collector will be well advised to take careful note of numbers which he may either recognize or discover; but he should use such notes as a guide, not as a bible.

Despite all these cautions, I believe that a copy of the 1932 catalogue constitutes the most valuable single document in the Lalique collector's library. It provides him with a rich supply of existing information, and with a challenge to seek for more.

□ *indicates that the object was made in clear glass.*
■ *indicates that the object was made in coloured glass.*
(a) *indicates that the object continued in production after the Second World War, manufactured by Cristal Lalique.*

Design No.		French description	English description

Boîtes et bonbonnières [boxes and sweet-dishes]

1	□	Boîte ronde, paon	*Known to exist in 1922*
2	□ ■	Boîte ronde, coq	
3	□ ■	Boîte ronde, amour assis	*Plate 139*
4	□ ■	Boîte ovale, roses en relief	
5	□	Boîte ronde, Louveciennes	*Two veiled dancers*
6	□	Boîte ronde, Ermenonville	*Veiled dancer with urn*
7	□	Boîte ronde, Fontenay	*Two naked dancers with flowers*
8			
9	□	Boîte ronde, 1 figurine et raisins	
10	□	Boîte ronde, 1 figurine et bouquets	
11	□	Boîte ronde, 2 figurines et branches	
12			
13			
14	□ ■	Boîte ronde, 4 papillons	
15	□ ■	Boîte ronde, 4 scarabées	
16			
17			
18			
19			
20	□	Boîte ovale, amours	
21	□	Boîte ovale, panier de roses	
22	□	Boîte ovale, Gabrielle	
23	□	Boîte ovale, cygnes	
24	□	Boîte ovale, 2 danseuses	
25			
26	□ ■	Boîte ronde, pommier du Japon	
27			
28	□	Boîte ronde, guirlande de graines	
29	■	Boîte ronde, houppes	
30	□	Boîte ronde, 3 paons	
31	□	Boîte ronde, Victoire	
32	□	Boîte ronde, 2 figurines	
33	□	Boîte ronde, 1 grand vase	
34	□	Boîte ronde, 2 pigeons	
35	□	Boîte ronde, 2 oiseaux	
36			
37	□	Boîte ronde, 3 vases	
38			
39	□	Boîte ronde, anges	
40			
41	■	Boîte ronde grande, muguets*	
42	■	Boîte ronde grande, cyprins*	*Plate 161*
43	■	Boîte ronde grande, 2 sirènes*	
44	■	Boîte ronde grande, cigales*	
45	■	Boîte ronde moyenne, Georgette*	*Three dragon-flies*
46	■	Boîte ronde moyenne, 3 dahlias*	
47	■	Boîte ronde moyenne, 6 dahlias*	
48			

* Could be supplied in either opaque or transparent glass.

Design No.		French description	English description
49	■	Boîte ronde petite, cléones	
50	■	Boîte ronde petite, Tokio	*Blossom*
51	■	Boîte ronde petite, libellules	
52	■	Boîte ronde petite, mésanges	*Six birds*
53	□	Boîte à cigarettes, hirondelles	*Rectangular*
54	□	Boîte à cigarettes, zinnias	*Rectangular*
55			
56			
57	□	Boîte ronde, Geneviève	*Feathers and two birds*
58	□	Boîte ronde, Compiègne	*Birds and foliage*
59	□	Boîte ronde, Fontainebleau	*Animals*
60	□	Boîte ronde, Rambouillet	
61	□	Boîte ronde, Meudon	*Flowers and leaves*
62	□	Boîte ronde, Chantilly	*Deer and foliage*
63	□	Boîte ronde, cheveux de Vénus	*Central finial on cover*
64	□	Boîte ronde, Isabelle	*Flowers*
65	□ ■	Boîte ronde, gui	
66	□	Boîte ronde, Degas	*Plate 168*
67	□	Boîte ronde, Lucie	*Forget-me-nots*
68	□	Boîte ronde, Vaucluse	*Leaves*
69	□	Boîte ronde, marguerites	*Plate 119*
70	□	Boîte ronde, Émiliane	*Flowers*
71	□ ■	Boîte ronde, coquilles	
72			
73			
74			
75	■	Boîte ronde, Roger	*Birds and foliage (known to exist in 1926)*
75	□	Boîte ronde, Roger, émaillé	*Plate 163*
76	□	Boîte hexagonale, Saint-Nectaire	*Swirl of leaves*
77	□ ■	Boîte ronde moyenne, primevères (160mm)	
78	□	Boîte ovale, Dinard	*Plate 78*
79	□	Boîte à cigares, Roméo (couvercle à glissière)	*Fluted*
80	□	Boîte à cigares, Corona	*Leaves*
81	■	Boîte ronde, Saint-Marc*	*Two birds*
82	□ ■	Boîte oeuf, pervenches	
83	□ ■	Boîte carrée, Sultane	*Seated nude*
84	□ ■	Boîte ronde, Vallauris	*Leaves with finial of berries*
85	□	Boîte oeuf, poussins	
86	□ ■	Boîte ronde grande, primevères (200mm)	*Plate 111*
87	□	Boîte carrée, palmettes	

(Numbers 88–149 not listed)

Buvards [hand blotters]

150	□	Buvard, grosses feuilles	
151	□	Buvard, escargots	
152	□	Buvard, cerises	
153	□	Buvard, faune et nymphe	
154	□	Buvard, 2 sirènes enlacées, assises	

* Could be supplied in either opaque or transparent glass.

Design No.		French description	English description
		French description	*English description*
155	□	Buvard, feuilles d'artichauds	
156	□	Buvard, mûres	*Plate 143*
157	□	Buvard, 2 sirènes face à face, couchées	

(Numbers 158–174 not listed)

Cachets [seals]

175	□ ■	Cachet, tête d'aigle		*Plate 15*
176	□	Cachet, 4 figurines, face		
177	□	Cachet, 4 figurines, angle		
178	□ ■	Cachet rond, bleuets		
179	□	Cachet, anneau, lézards		
180	□	Cachet, mouche		
181	□ ■	Cachet, statuette drapée		
182	□ ■	Cachet, poisson		
183	□ ■	Cachet, sauterelle		
184	□	Cachet, motif aigle (bouchon d'encrier)		
185	□	Cachet, motif souris (bouchon d'encrier)		
186	□	Cachet, motif pigeon (bouchon d'encrier)		
187	□	Cachet, perruches		
188	□	Cachet, hirondelles		
189	□	Cachet, vase de fleurs		
190	□	Cachet, papillon, ailes fermées		
191				
192	□	Cachet, papillon, ailes ouvertes		
193	□	Cachet rond, figurine dans les fleurs		
194	□	Cachet rond, 2 danseuses		
195	□	Cachet, armes d'Angleterre		
196	□ ■	Cachet, double marguerite		
197	□	Cachet rond, 3 papillons		
198	□	Cachet rond, 2 perruches et fleurs		
199				
200	□	Cachet rond, 2 figurines et fleurs		
201	□	Cachet ovale, figurine ailée		
202	□	Cachet ovale, figurine		
203				
204				
205				
206				
207				
208				
209	□ ■	Cachet, figurine mains jointes		
210	□ ■	Cachet, victoire		
211	□	Cachet ovale, sirènes		
212	□	Cachet ovale, fuchsias		
213	□	Cachet rond, cigognes		
214	□ ■	Cachet, lapin		
215	□ ■	Cachet, dindon		
216	□ ■	Cachet, chien		
217	□ ■	Cachet, renard		
218	□ ■	Cachet souris		
219	□ ■	Cachet, canard		

Design		
No.	*French description*	*English description*
220 □ ■	Cachet, moineau	
221 □ ■	Cachet, naïade	*Nude woman etched on plaque.*
		Plate 142
222 □ ■	Cachet, pélican	
223 □ ■	Cachet, pinson	
224 □ ■	Cachet, caravelle	
225 □	Cachet, bélier	
226 □	Cachet, chamois	
227 □ ■	Cachet, écureuil	
228 □	Cachet, faune	
229 □	Cachet, athlètes	
230 □ ■	Cachet, 2 colombes	
231 □	Cachet, Nice	

(Numbers 232–249 not listed)

Cadres [picture frames]

250 □	Cadre, 2 figurines et fleurs	
251		
252		
253 □ ■	Cadre, muguets	
254 □	Cadre, bleuets	
255 □	Cadre, Laurea	*Pattern of interlacing lines*
256 □ ■	Cadre, bergeronettes	*Birds and fruit*
257 □ ■	Cadre, hirondelles	*Known to have existed in 1926*
258 □ ■	Cadre, inséparables	*Love birds in couples*
		amongst branches
259 □ ■	Cadre, étoiles	
260 □ ■	Cadre, lys	
261		
262		
263 □ ■	Cadre, guirlandes	
264 □	Cadre, naïades	

(Numbers 265–274 not listed)

Cendriers [ashtrays]

275 □ ■	Cendrier rond, 2 zéphyrs
276	
277	
278 □ ■	Cendrier rond, archers
279 □ ■	Cendrier ovale, feuilles
280 □ ■	Cendrier ovale, Médicis
281 □ ■	Cendrier carré, Vézelay
282 □ ■	Cendrier octog., fauvettes
283 □ ■	Cendrier rond, canard
284 □ ■	Cendrier rond, moineau
285 □ ■	Cendrier rond, lapin
286 □ ■	Cendrier rond, souris
287 □ ■	Cendrier rond, dindon
288 □ ■	Cendrier rond, statuette de la fontaine

Design No.			French description	English description
289	□	■	Cendrier octog., Alice	
290	□	■	Cendrier rond, chien	
291	□	■	Cendrier rond, Renard	
292	□		Cendrier rond, Trianon	
293	□	■	Cendrier rond, Anthéor	
294	□	■	Cendrier rond, Cuba	
295	□	■	Cendrier rond, Tabago	
296	□	■	Cendrier rond, Jamaïque	*(a)*
297	□	■	Cendrier rond, Grenade	
298	□	■	Cendrier rond, Martinique	
299	□	■	Cendrier rond, Pâquerette	
300	□	■	Cendrier rond, Simone	
301	□	■	Cendrier rond, Louise	
302	□	■	Cendrier rond, Berthe	
303	□	■	Cendrier carré, Anna	
304	□	■	Cendrier rond, Irène	
305	□	■	Cendrier rond, Nicole	
306	□		Cendrier carré, Marsan	
307	□	■	Cendrier carré, Varèse	
308	□	■	Cendrier rond, Sumatra	
309	□	■	Cendrier rond, naïade	*(a)*
310	□	■	Cendrier rond, pélican	
311	□	■	Cendrier rond, pinson	*(a)*
312	□	■	Cendrier rond, caravelle	*(a)*
313	□		Cendrier rond, bélier	
314	□		Cendrier rond, chamois	
315	□	■	Cendrier rond, écureuil	*(a)*
316	□		Cendrier rond, faune	
317	□		Cendrier rond, dahlia	
318	□		Cendrier rond, dahlia et papillon	
319	□		Cendrier rond, athlètes	
320	□	■	Cendrier rond, 2 colombes	*(a)*

(Numbers 321–349 not listed)

Coffrets [boxes]

350	□		Coffret, monnaie du pape, 5 plaques	
351	□		Coffret, papillons, 5 plaques	
352				
353	□		Coffret, monnaie du pape, 1 plaque	
354	□		Coffret, papillons, 1 plaque	
355	□		Coffret, chrysanthèmes, 1 plaque	
356	□		Coffret, figurines, 5 plaques	

(Numbers 357–374 not listed)

Coupes et Assiettes [bowls and plates]

375	□	■	Coupe sirènes	
376	□	■	Coupe trépied, sirène	
377	□	■	Coupe, Martigues	*Golfish design. Plate 21. (a)*
378		■	Coupe, cyprins, plate	*Goldfish design*

Design No.		French description	English description
379	□ ■	Coupe, cyprins, refermée	
380	□ ■	Coupe, ondines, ouverte	
381	□ ■	Coupe, ondines, fermée	
382	□ ■	Coupe, lys, satiné	*Tripod. Plate 82*
383	□ ■	Coupe, volubilis	*Pattern of leaves*
384			
385	□ ■	Coupe, vasque, coquilles	*Plate 2*
386			
387	□ ■	Coupe sur pied, Clairvaux, émail	*Single-stemmed bowl*
388	□ ■	Coupe sur pied, Saint-Denis, émail	*Single-stemmed bowl. Plate 171*
389	□ ■	Coupe, filix	
389	□ ■	Coupe, filix, émail	
390	□ ■	Coupe, gazelles	
391	□ ■	Coupe, Saint-Vincent	*Pattern of grape and vines*
392	□ ■	Coupe, Cernuschi	*A deep bowl with a design in relief round the rim*
393	□ ■	Coupe, Armentières	*Bowl with a border of roses round the rim*
394			
395	■	Coupe, Vernon	*Three large flowers*
396	■	Coupe, Mont-Dore	*Wreath*
397	■	Coupe, Véronique	*Three Veronica blossoms*
398	■	Coupe, nonnettes	*Birds with outspread wings in three groups*
399	□ ■	Coupe, Montigny	*Geometric pattern*
400	□ ■	Coupe, Crémieu	*Geometric design of ropes and bubbles*
401	□ ■	Coupe, Tournon	*A silver-rimmed vase with flower design*
402	□ ■	Coupe, Villeneuve	*Star design*
403	□ ■	Coupe, Madagascar	*Border of monkey heads. Plate 41*
404	□ ■	Coupe, Nemours, émail	*Design of flowers with enamel centres, covering bowl. (a)*
405	□ ■	Coupe, Fleurville	*Several borders of flowers*
406	■	Coupe, phalènes	*Plate 4*
407	■	Coupe, Flora Bella	*Design of blossoms*
408	■	Coupe, Anvers	*Pattern of plant stems and pods in border*
409	■	Coupe, rosace	*Geometric arrangement of triangles*
410	■	Coupe, anges	
411	□	Coupe, éléphants	*Border of elephants in relief. Plates 39 and 40*
412	□	Coupe cristal, 2 moineaux moqueurs	*(a)*
413	□ ■	Coupe, Calypso	*Nude sea nymphs*
414	□ ■	Assiette, Calypso	
415	□ ■	Assiette, églantine	*Flowers in relief in centre of plate*

(Numbers 416–424 not listed)

Design No.		French description	English description

Encriers [inkwells]

425	□ ■	Encrier, nénuphar	
426	□ ■	Encrier, 3 papillons	
427	□ ■	Encrier, biches	
428	□	Encrier plateau, aigle	*Plate 86*
429	□	Encrier plateau, souris	
430	□	Encrier plateau, pigeons	
431	□ ■	Encrier rond, mûres	
432	□ ■	Encrier rond, serpents	
433	□ ■	Encrier rond, escargots	
434	□ ■	Encrier rond, 4 sirènes	
435			
436			
437	□ ■	Encrier rond, Cernay	
438	□	Encrier rectang., Colbert (50 épreuves)	*A limited edition of 50*
439	□ ■	Encrier rectang., Sully	
440	□ ■	Encrier rectang., Mirabeau (couvercle à glissière)	

(Numbers 441–474 not listed)

Flacons [flasks]

475	□ ■	Flacon, 4 cigales	*Tall, rectangular bottle with four moulded cicada*
476	□	Flacon, pavot	*Small rounded bottle moulded with a design of the petals of a poppy, and decorative moulded stopper*
477	□	Flacon, bouchon papillons	*Rounded squat bottle with moulded butterflies on stopper.*
478	□	Flacon, petites feuilles	
479			
480			
481			
482	□	Flacon, lunaria	
483	□	Flacon, olives	
484	□	Flacon, capricorne	*Engraved and enamelled scarabs on bottle and round flat top*
485	□	Flacon, lentilles	
486	□	Flacon, fleurs concaves	*Plate 108*
487	□	Flacon, panier de roses	*A pattern of trellis-work over the vase-shaped bottle with moulded roses in a border at the top and on stopper*
488	□	Flacon, rosace figurines	*A round bottle with a design of nude figures and a fan-like moulded stopper*
489	□	Flacon, fougères, bustes de femmes	*A tiny rectangular bottle with a moulded pattern of ferns and an oval medallion of a bust of a woman with a mirror*

Design No.		French description	English description
490	□	Flacon, méplat, 2 figurines, bouchons figurines	*A thin rectangular bottle with an oval panel containing two nude figures and a moulded figure on the stopper*
491	□ ■	Flacon, salamandres	
492	□	Flacon, nénuphar	
493	□	Flacon, bouchon fleurs du pommier	*Plate 103*
494	□ ■	Flacon, bouchon cassis	*A panelled bottle with grapes on the stopper*
495	□ ■	Flacon, bouchon mûres	*A rectangular panelled bottle with mulberries on the stopper*
496	□	Flacon, bouchon, 3 hirondelles	*A plain bottle with three swallows on the stopper*
497	□	Flacon, spirales	
498	□	Flacon, 3 guêpes	
499	□	Flacon, anses et bouchon marguerites	
500	□	Flacon, collerette, glands de soie	
501	□	Flacon, gros fruits, glands de soie	
502	□	Flacon, serpent	*An oval flask with a moulded snake's skin pattern and a snake-shaped stopper*
503	□	Flacon carré, hirondelles	*Plate 116*
504	□	Flacon, Pan	*A bottle with four moulded heads of Pan and leafy ornamentation*
505	□	Flacon, 4 soleils	
506	□	Flacon, Lepage	
507	□ ■	Flacon, bouchon eucalyptus	*A thin flask with a stopper of eucalyptus pods and leaves*
508	□ ■	Flacon, telline	*A clam-shaped flask with a stopper in the form of a shell. Plate 106*
509			
510	□	Flacon, carnette fleurs	
511	□	Flacon plat, 3 groupes de 2 danseuses	
512	□	Flacon plat, 6 danseuses	
513	□	Flacon, glycines	
514	□ ■	Flacon, Amphritite	*A bottle moulded and engraved in the form of a snail shell with a stopper in the shape of a kneeling nude*
515	□ ■	Flacon, Marquita	
516	□ ■	Flacon, Camille	
517	□ ■	Flacon, Clamart	
518	□	Flacon, Palerme	
519	□ ■	Flacon, cactus	*(a)*
520	□ ■	Flacon, Amélie	
521	□ ■	Flacon, Grégoire	
522	□ ■	Flacon, Hélène (Lotus)	*Lotus leaves and seed pods on a small squat flask. Plate 115*
523	□ ■	Flacon, Ambroise	
524	□ ■	Flacon, Tantot	*A moulded design of leaves on a tall, oval bottle and its stopper*
525	□	Flacon, muguet	*A small flask with a stopper in the shape of a bunch of lilies*

Design No.			French description	English description
526	□		Flacon, Clairefontaine	*A small circular flask with lilies of the valley on the stopper*

(Numbers 527–574 not listed)

Garnitures de Toilette [dressing table sets]
Throughout this section ■ denotes an enamel finish

575	□	■	Fleurettes, flacon No 1 *	*Plate 111*
576	□	■	Fleurettes, flacon No 2 *	
577	□	■	Fleurettes, flacon No 3 *	
578	□	■	Fleurettes, polissoir *	
579	□	■	Fleurettes, épinglier *	
580	□	■	Fleurettes, boîte à poudre *, haute no 1	
581	□	■	Fleurettes, boîte à poudre *, basse No 2	
582	□	■	Fleurettes, coupe à peignes *	
583	□	■	Fleurettes, porte-savon *	
584	□	■	Fleurettes, bol à éponge *	
585				
586				
587				
588				
589				
590	□	■	Épines, flacon No 1	
591	□	■	Épines, flacon No 2	
592	□	■	Épines, flacon No 3	
593	□	■	Épines, flacon No 4	*Plate 117*
594	□	■	Épines, boîte No 1	
595	□	■	Épines, boîte No 2	
596	□	■	Épines, boîte No 3	
597	□	■	Épines, épinglier	
598	□	■	Épines, coupe à peignes	
599	□	■	Épines, porte-savon	
600	□	■	Perles, flacon No 1, satiné	
600	□		Perles, flacon No 1, poli	
601	□		Perles, flacon No 2, satiné	
601	□		Perles, flacon No 2, poli	*Plate 105*
602	□	■	Perles, flacon No 3, satiné	
602	□	■	Perles, flacon No 3, poli	
603	□	■	Perles, boîte No 1, satiné	
603	□		Perles, boîte No 1, poli	
604	□	■	Perles, boîte No 2, satiné	
604	□		Perles, boîte No 2, poli	
605	□	■	Perles, coupe à peignes, satiné	
605	□		Perles, coupe à peignes, poli	
606	□	■	Perles, porte-savon, satiné	
606	□		Perles, porte-savon, poli	
607	□	■	Perles, épinglier, satiné	
607	□		Perles, épinglier, poli	
608	□	■	Perles, bol à éponge, satiné	
608	□		Perles, bol à éponge, poli	
609	□	■	Enfants, flacon	*(a)*

* Could be supplied in satin or transparent glass.

Design No.		French description	English description
610	□ ■	Enfants, boîte	*(a)*
611	□ ■	Myosotis (bouchon figurine), flacon No 1	
612	□ ■	Myosotis (bouchon figurine), flacon No 2	
613	□ ■	Myosotis (bouchon figurine), flacon No 3	
614	□ ■	Myosotis (bouchon figurine), boîte No 1	
615	□ ■	Dahlia, flacon No 1	*Plate 110. (a)*
616	□ ■	Dahlia, flacon No 2	*(a)*
617	□ ■	Dahlia, flacon No 3	*(a)*
618	□ ■	Dahlia, flacon No 4	*(a)*
619	□ ■	Dahlia, boîte No 1	*(a)*
620	□ ■	Dahlia, boîte No 2	*(a)*
621			
622			
623	□ ■	Duncan, flacon No 1	*(a)*
624	□ ■	Duncan, flacon No 2	*(a)*
625	□ ■	Duncan, flacon No 3	*(a)*
626	□ ■	Duncan, flacon No 4	*(a)*
627	□ ■	Duncan, boîte No 1	*(a)*
628	□ ■	Duncan, boîte No 2	*(a)*
629	□ ■	Duncan, épinglier	*(a)*
630	□ ■	Duncan, coupe à peignes	*(a)*
631	□ ■	Duncan, bol à éponge	*(a)*

(Numbers 632–649 not listed)

Vaporisateurs [scent sprays]

Design No.		French description	English description
650	□ ■	Épines, flacon No 1	
651	□ ■	Épines, flacon No 2	
652	□ ■	Épines, flacon No 3	
653	□ ■	Épines, flacon No 4	
654	□ ■	Fleurettes, No 1	
655	□ ■	Fleurettes, No 2	
656	□ ■	Fleurettes, No 3	
657	□ ■	Perles No 1, satiné	
657	□	Perles No 1, poli	
658	□ ■	Perles No 2, satiné	
658	□	Perles No 2, poli	
659	□ ■	Perles No 3, satiné	
659	□	Perles No 3, poli	
660	□ ■	Sirénes	
661			
662	□ ■	Mimosa	
663	□ ■	Enfants	*(a)*
664	□ ■	Dahlia, flacon No 2	*(a)*
665	□ ■	Dahlia, flacon No 3	*(a)*
666	□ ■	Dahlia, flacon No 4	*(a)*
667	□ ■	Duncan	*(a)*

(Numbers 668–674 not listed)

Design No.		*French description*	*English description*

Miroirs [mirrors]

675	□	Miroir, Narcisse couché	
676			
677	□	Miroir rond, 2 oiseaux	*Plate 150*
678	□	Miroir rond, 2 chèvres	
679	□	Miroir rond, 3 paons, gland de soie	
680	□	Miroir ovale, sauterelles	
681	□	Miroir ovale, Psyché	
682	□	Miroir ovale, tête	
683	□	Miroir ovale, Narcisse debout	
684	□	Miroir rond, muguets, gland de soie	
685	□	Miroir rond grand, églantines	*Frontispiece*
686	□	Miroir rond, épines, grand	

(Numbers 686–724 not listed)

Pendules [clocks]

725	□ ■	Pendule, électrique, feuilles	
726	□	Pendule, électrique, 2 figurines	
727	□ ■	Pendule, électrique, 2 colombes	
728	■	Pendule, électrique, le jour et la nuit	
729	□ ■	Pendule, électrique, sirènes	
730			
731	□	Pendule, 8 jours, roitelets	
732	□	Pendule, 8 jours, papillons	
733	□	Pendule, 8 jours, muguet	*A round glass case with a border engraved with lilies of the valley*
734	□	Pendule, 8 jours, Marly, émail	*A small circular clock case with sprays of lily of the valley*
735	□	Pendule, 8 jours, rossignols	*A round glass clock case on a glass base with nightingales to mark the hours*
736	□	Pendule, 8 jours, Hélène	*A rectangular clock decorated with flower garlands and three nudes on the pediment*

(Numbers 737–759 not listed)

Pendulettes [small clocks]

760	□	Pendulette, 8 jours, 4 perruches	
761	□	Pendulette, 8 jours, 5 hirondelles	
762	□	Pendulette, 8 jours, marguerites	
763	□	Pendulette, 8 jours, 6 hirondelles	
764	■	Pendulette, 8 jours, naïades	*Plate 146*
765	■	Pendulette, 8 jours, inséparables	*Plate 147*
766	□	Pendulette, 8 jours, pierrots	
767	□	Pendulette, 8 jours, Antoinette	

(Numbers 768–800 not listed)

Design No.	French description	English description

Presse-papiers [paper-weights]

801 ☐ ■	Presse-papiers, 2 aigles	*Plate 97*
802 ☐ ■	Presse-papiers, double marguerite	
803 ☐	Presse-papiers, 2 sardines	
804 ☐	Presse-papiers, 3 sardines	

(Numbers 805–825 not listed)

Statuettes

826 ☐ ■	Statuette, joueuse de flûte	
827 ☐ ■	Statuette, tête penchée	*A figure enclosed in an oval of glass with floral decoration in relief*
828 ☐ ■	Statuette voilée, mains jointes	
829 ☐ ■	Statuette moyenne, voilée	
830 ☐ ■	Statuette moyenne, nue	*Plate 145*
831 ☐ ■	Statuette, sirène	*Plate 141*
832 ☐ ■	Statuette, naïade	*Plate 140*
833 ☐ ■	Statuette, Suzanne	
833 ☐ ■	Statuette, Suzanne, sur socle bronze, monture électr.	*Plate 13*
834 ☐ ■	Statuette, Thaïs	
834 ☐ ■	Statuette, Thaïs sur socle bronze monture électr.	
835 ☐	Statuette, nue, bras levés	
835 ☐	Statuette, nue, bras levés, sur socle bois, monture électrique	
836 ☐ ■	Statuette, socle lierre, sur socle bois	
837 ☐	Statuette, source de la fontaine	
838 ☐	Statuette, source de la fontaine	
839 ☐	Statuette, source de la fontaine	
840 ☐	Statuette, source de la fontaine	
841 ☐	Statuette, source de la fontaine	*Different sizes of statuette based on caryatids from fountain at 1925 Exhibition (see Chapter 9)*
842 ☐	Statuette, source de la fontaine	
843 ☐	Statuette, source de la fontaine	
844 ☐	Statuette, source de la fontaine	
845 ☐	Statuette, source de la fontaine	
846 ☐	Statuette, source de la fontaine	
847 ☐	Statuette, source de la fontaine	
848 ☐	Statuette, source de la fontaine	
849 ☐	Statuette, source de la fontaine	

(Numbers 850–874 not listed)

Vases

875 ☐ ■	Vase, antilopes, émaillé	
876 ☐ ■	Vase, perruches	*Vase with groups of paired parakeets in branches*
877 ☐ ■	Vase, grande boule, lierre	*Spherical vase with a design of ivy leaves*

Design No.		French description	English description
878	□ ■	Vase, 4 masques	*Short-necked vase with four medallions and foliage*
879			
880	□ ■	Vase, 2 anneaux, pigeons	
881	□ ■	Vase, 2 anneaux, lézards	
882	□ ■	Vase, 2 anneaux, scarabées	
883	□ ■	Vase, méplat, sirènes, avec bouchon figurine	
884			
885			
886	□ ■	Vase, 6 figurines et masques	
887			
888			
889			
890	□ ■	Vase, lutteurs	
891	□ ■	Vase camées	
892	□ ■	Vase, gros scarabées	*Spherical vase with beetles on relief and a short neck*
893	□ ■	Vase, archers	*An oval vase with short neck and a design in relief of nude males hunting birds. Plate 37*
894	□ ■	Vase, baies	
894	□ ■	Vase, baies, émaillé	
895			
896	□ ■	Vase, serpent	
897	□ ■	Vase, monnaie du pape	
898			
899			
900	□ ■	Vase, courges	
901	□ ■	Vase, poivre	
902	□ ■	Vase, acanthes	
903	□ ■	Vase, gobelet, 6 figurines	
904	□ ■	Vase, béliers	
905	□ ■	Vase, Ceylan (8 perruches)	*Plate 33*
906	□ ■	Vase, fontaine, couvert	
907	□	Vase, bordure bleuets	
908	□	Vase, bordure épines	
909	□	Vase, bleuets	
910			
911	□ ■	Vase, 2 moineaux dormant	
912	□ ■	Vase, 2 moineaux bavardant	
913			
914	□ ■	Vase, 12 figurines avec bouchon figurine	
915	□ ■	Vase cristal, 2 sauterelles	
916			
917			
918			
919	□ ■	Vase, aras	
920	□ ■	Vase, martins pêcheurs	
921	□	Vase, épicea	
922			
923			
924	□	Vase, cariatides, couvert	

Design No.		French description	English description
925	□ ■	Vase, poissons	*Plate 62*
926	□	Vase, soleil, émaillé	
927			
928			
929	□ ■	Vase, chardons	
930	□ ■	Vase, voilettes	
931	□ ■	Vase, escargot	
932	□ ■	Vase, coquilles	
933			
934	□ ■	Vase, Formose	*Known to have existed in 1925. Plate 16*
935	□ ■	Vase, sauge	
936	□ ■	Vase, eucalyptus	*Plate 29*
937	□ ■	Vase, Druides	*Emerald green vase with a mistletoe design*
938	□ ■	Vase, dahlias	*Plate 60*
939			
940	□ ■	Vase, néfliers	
941	□ ■	Vase, Estérel	
942	□ ■	Vase, lièvres	
943	□ ■	Vase, dentelé	
944	□ ■	Vase, plumes	
945	□	Vase, lotus	
946			
947			
948	□ ■	Vase, gui	*Plate 23*
949	□ ■	Vase, acacia	
950	□	Vase, méduse	
951	□	Vase, guirlande de roses, mat	
952	□ ■	Vase, palmes	
953	□	Vase, mimosa	
954	□ ■	Vase, églantines	
955	□	Vase, Téhéran (genre gravure)	
956	□ ■	Vase, Tournai	*Plate 51*
957	□ ■	Vase, Malines	
958	□ ■	Vase, Albert	
959	□ ■	Vase, perles	
960	□ ■	Vase, Beaulieu (décor gravé)	
961	■	Vase, Cluny (anses bronze)	*Spherical vase with bronze handles*
962	■	Vase, Senlis (anses bronze)	*Spherical vase with bronze handles of stylized leaves*
963	□ ■	Vase, tourterelles	
964	□ ■	Vase, oranges, émaillé	*Spherical vase with design of oranges and leaves*
965			
966	□ ■	Vase, tortues	*An oval vase with short neck and an overall design of tortoises*
967	□	Vase, Lagamar, émaillé	
968	□	Vase, Koudour	
969	□	Vase, Morgan	
970	□	Vase, Nimroud	
971			

Design No.			*French description*	*English description*
972	□	■	Vase, Danaïdes	*Known to have existed in 1926. Plate 36*
973		■	Vase, tourbillons	*Plate 31*
973	□		Vase, tourbillons, émaillé	*Known to have existed in 1926*
974	□	■	Vase, Chamaraude	*Plate 54*
975	□	■	Vase, Yvelines	
976	□	■	Vase, Ornis	*Known to have existed in 1926. Plate 56*
977	□	■	Vase, sophora	*A spherical vase with a short neck and design in leafy vine. Plate 56*
978	□		Vase, charmilles	*Known to have existed in 1926*
979				*Vase with thistle design*
980	□	■	Vase, Palissy	
981	□	■	Vase, Bouchardon	
982	□	■	Vase, Ronsard	
983				
984	□	■	Vase, ormeaux	
985				
986	□	■	Vase, Avallon	
987	□	■	Vase, grimperaux	
988	□	■	Vase, aigrettes	
989	□	■	Vase, Beautreillis	
990	□	■	Vase, Pierrefonds	*Large open-scrolled handles. Plate 28*
991	□	■	Vase, Rampillon	*Plate 30*
992	□	■	Vase, Moissac	*Silver-rimmed; known to have existed in 1925. Plate 24*
993	□	■	Vase, Bellecour	*Four birds round neck*
994	□		Vase, Honfleur	
995	□	■	Vase, tulipes	
996				*Moulded figures of nudes round straight-sided vase*
997	□	■	Vase, bacchantes	*Plate 19. (a)*
998	□	■	Vase, Alicante	*Parrot heads in relief*
999	□	■	Vase, Oran	
1000	□	■	Vase, Armorique	
1001	□	■	Vase, Dordogne	
1002	□	■	Vase, Marisa	
1003	□	■	Vase, Périgord	
1004	□	■	Vase, Champagne	
1005	□	■	Vase, Nivernais	
1006	□	■	Vase, Picardie	
1007	□	■	Vase, tournesol	
1008	□	■	Vase, Oléron	
1009				
1010	□	■	Vase, Cameret	
1011	□	■	Vase, Penthièvre	
1012				
1013	□	■	Vase, Tristan	
1014				
1015	□	■	Vase, Salmonides	
1016	□	■	Vase, Soudan	

Design No.			French description	English description
1017	□	■	Vase, Borromée	
1018				
1019	□	■	Vase, Ferrières	*Plate 49*
1020	□		Vase, Caudebec	
1021	□	■	Vase, Languedoc	
1022	□	■	Vase, Montargis	
1023	□	■	Vase, Amiens	*Plate 53*
1024	□	■	Vase, Pétrarque	*Plate 27*
1025	□	■	Vase, Milan	
1026	□		Vase à tulipes, Delft	
1027	□		Vase à tulipes, Rotterdam	
1028	□		Vase à tulipes, Breda	
1029	□		Vase à tulipes, Utrecht	
1030	□	■	Vase, Margaret	
1031	□	■	Vase, Sylvia, couvert	
1032	□	■	Vase, raisins	
1033	□	■	Vase, coqs et plumes	
1034	□	■	Vase, coqs et raisins	*Plate 34*
1035	□	■	Vase, cerises	
1036	□	■	Vase, Fontainebleau	*Plate 46*
1037	□	■	Vase, prunes	*Plate 45*
1038	□	■	Vase, pinsons	
1039	□	■	Vase, soucis	
1040	□	■	Vase, lilas	
1041	□	■	Vase, lierre	
1042	□	■	Vase, graines	
1043	□	■	Vase, Piriac	
1044	□	■	Vase, renoncules	
1045	□	■	Vase, grenade	
1046				
1047	□	■	Vase, chevaux	
1048	□	■	Vase, Naïades	
1049	□	■	Vase, Monaco	
1050	□	■	Vase, Montmorency	
1051	□	■	Vase, Carthage	
1052	□	■	Vase, farandole	
1053	□	■	Vase, Tuileries	
1054	□	■	Vase, Nadica	
1055	□	■	Vase, Saint François	
1056	□		Vase, Bornéo, émail	
1057	□		Vase, couvercle chrysanthème, socle bois	
1058	□	■	Vase, mûres	
1059	□		Vase, Bali	
1060	□	■	Vase, spirales	*Plate 44*
1061	□		Vase à tulipes, Helder	
1062	□		Vase, faune, taillé	
1063	□		Vase, grillons, taillé	
1064	□		Vase, mésangers, taillé	
1065	□		Vase, roitelets, taillé	
1066	□		Vase, 2 pigeons, taillé	
1067	□		Vase, écureuils, taillé	
1068	□		Vase, coq, taillé	

Design No.		French description	English description
1069	□	Vase, Beauvais, taillé	
1070	□	Vase, enfants	
1071	□	Vase, merles, taillé	
1072	■	Vase, laiterons	
1073	■	Vase, Bresse	
1074	■	Vase, Le Mans	
1075	■	Vase, chamois	
1076	■	Vase, canards	

(Numbers 1077–1099 not listed)

Motifs décoratifs [ornaments]

1100	□ ■	Gros poisson, vagues	
1100	□ ■	Gros poisson, vagues, sur socle bronze	*Plate 125*
1101	□ ■	Gros poisson, algues	
1101	□ ■	Gros poisson, algues, sur socle bronze, monture électrique	
1102			
1103			
1104			
1105			
1106	□	Motif hirondelles, socle verre	
1107	□	Motif hirondelles, socle bronze	
1107	□	Motif hirondelles, socle bronze seul	
1108	□	Motif 4 danseuses, socle bronze	
1108	□	Motif 4 danseuses, socle bronze, mont. électr.	
1109	□	Surtout, 2 cavaliers, socle bronze, mont. électr.	*Plate 124*
1110	□	Surtout, 3 paons, socle bronze, mont. électr.	*Plate 124*
1111		Oiseau de feu	
1111	□	Oiseau de feu, socle bronze, mont. électr.	
1112			
1113			
1114			
1115			
1116			
1117			
1118			
1119			
1120			
1121		Gobelet, porte-cigarette, lierre	*Listed under 'Divers'*
1122	□	Bouchon de radiateur, 5 chevaux	*Plates 10 and 85*
1123	□	Bouchon de radiateur, comète	*Plate 89*
1124	□	Bouchon de radiateur, faucon	*Plate 87*
1125	□	Support coriatide	*Listed under 'Divers'*
1126	□	Bouchon de radiateur, archer	*Also listed under 'Presse-papiers'. Plate 83*

Design No.	French description	English description

Presse-papiers [paper-weights]

Design No.		French description	English description
1127			
1128	□ ■	Presse-papiers, 2 tourterelles	
1129			
1130			
1131			
1132			
1133			
1134			
1135	□ ■	Presse-papiers, coq nain	*Also listed under 'Bouchon de radiateur'. Plate 94. (a)*
1136	□	Presse-papiers, tête de bélier	*Also listed under 'Bouchon de radiateur'. Plate 101*
1137	□	Presse-papiers, tête de coq	*Also listed under 'Bouchon de radiateur'*
1138	□	Presse-papiers, tête d'aigle	*Also listed under 'Bouchon de radiateur'. Plate 14*
1139	□ ■	Presse-papiers, tête d'épervier	*Also listed under 'Bouchon de radiateur'. Plate 102*
1140	□ ■	Presse-papiers, tête de paon	*Also listed under 'Bouchon de radiateur'. Plate 92*
1141	□ ■	Presse-papiers, levrier	*Also listed under 'Bouchon de radiateur'*
1142	□ ■	Presse-papiers, St Christopher	*Also listed under 'Bouchon de radiateur'. Plate 99*
1143	□	Presse-papiers, hirondelle	*Also listed under 'Bouchon de radiateur'. Plate 88. (a)*
1144	□	Presse-papiers, libellule, petite	*Also listed under 'Bouchon de radiateur'. Plate 100*
1145	□	Presse-papiers, libellule, grande	*Also listed under 'Bouchon de radiateur'. Plate 90*
1146	□ ■	Presse-papiers, grenouille	*Also listed under 'Bouchon de radiateur'. Plate 93*
1147	□	Presse-papiers, Victoire	*Also listed under 'Bouchon de radiateur'. Plate 95*
1148	□ ■	Presse-papiers, antilope	*Also listed under 'Motif décoratif'*
1149	□	Presse-papiers, moineau fier	*Also listed under 'Motif décoratif'*
1150	□	Presse-papiers, moineau hardi	*Also listed under 'Motif décoratif'*
1151	□	Presse-papiers, moineau timide	*Also listed under 'Motif décoratif'*
1152	□	Presse-papiers, Longchamps	*Also listed under 'Bouchon de radiateur'*
1153	□	Presse-papiers, Epsom	*Also listed under 'Bouchon de radiateur'. Plate 91*
1154	□	Presse-papiers, moineau sur socle (ailes croisées)	*Also listed under 'Motif décoratif'*
1155	□	Presse-papiers, moineau sur socle (ailes ouvertes)	*Also listed under 'Motif décoratif'*
1156	□	Presse-papiers, moineau sur socle (ailes fermées)	*Also listed under 'Motif décoratif'*
1157	□ ■	Presse-papiers, sanglier	*Also listed under 'Bouchon de radiateur'. Plate 96*

Design No.		French description	English description
1158	☐ ■	Presse-papiers, perche	*Also listed under 'Bouchon de radiateur'. (a)*
1159	☐ ■	Presse-papiers, cheval	*Also listed under 'Bouchon de radiateur'.*
1160	☐ ■	Presse-papiers, vitesse	*Also listed under 'Bouchon de radiateur'.*
1161	☐ ■	Presse-papiers, coq Houdan	
1162	☐ ■	Presse-papiers, chat	
1163	☐ ■	Serre-livres, amours	*Listed under 'Divers'*
1164	☐	Presse-papiers, pintade	*Also listed under 'Bouchon de radiateur'*
1165	☐	Presse-papiers, moineau coquet	*Also listed under 'Motif décoratif'*
1166	☐	Presse-papiers, moineau sournois	*Also listed under 'Motif décoratif'*
1167	☐	Presse-papiers, moineau moqueur	*Also listed under 'Motif décoratif'*
1168	☐ ■	Presse-papiers, daim	

Motifs décoratifs [ornaments]

1169	☐	Surtout, caravelle	*Plate 120*
1170	☐	Surtout, Yéso (poissons)	
1171	☐	Surtout, fauvettes A	
1172	☐	Surtout, fauvettes B	
1173	☐	Surtout, fauvettes C	
1174	☐	Surtout, nid d'oiseaux	
1175	☐	Surtout, amours	
1176	☐	Presse-papiers, barbillons	
1177	☐	Surtout, tulipes	
1178	☐	Vase, 2 anémones	
1179	☐	Anémone ouverte	
1180	☐	Anémone fermée	
1181	☐	Presse-papiers, hibou	*Also listed under 'Bouchon de radiateur'*
1182	☐	Presse-papiers, renards	*Also listed under 'Bouchon de radiateur'*
1183	☐	Bouchon de radiateur, Chrysis	*Also listed under 'Motif décoratif'. Plate 98. (a)*

Caves à Liqueurs [tantaluses]

1184	■	Cave à Liqueurs, pan et bacchantes
1185	■	Cave à Liqueurs, flacon seul, pan
1186	■	Cave à Liqueurs, flacon seul, bacchantes
1187	■	Cave à Liqueurs, enfant
1188	■	Cave à Liqueurs, flacon seul
1189	■	Cave à Liqueurs, vigne
1190	■	Cave à Liqueurs, flacon seul

Presse-papiers [paper-weights]

1191	☐	Presse-papiers, éléphant	*(a)*
1192	☐	Presse-papiers, Toby (éléphant)	
1193	☐	Presse-papiers, chouette	

Design No.		*French description*	*English description*
1194	☐	Presse-papiers, taureau	*(a)*
1195	☐	Presse-papiers, rhinocéros	*Plate 84*
1196	☐	Presse-papiers, bison	*(a)*
1197	☐	Presse-papiers, renne	
1198	☐	Christ	*Listed under 'Divers'*
1198	☐	Christ, sur socle chrome	*Listed under 'Divers'*
1198	☐	Christ, sur socle bois	*Listed under 'Divers'*
1199	☐	Pigeon Liège	*Listed under 'Motifs décoratifs'*
1200	☐	Pigeon Namur	*Listed under 'Motifs décoratifs'*
1201	■	Cave à Liqueurs, Glascow	
1202	■	Cave à Liqueurs, flacon seul	

(Numbers 1203–1325 not listed)

Bracelets

1326	☐ ■	Bracelet extensible, 25 rondelles, dahlias
1327	☐ ■	Bracelet extensible, 32 rondelles, zig-zag
1328	☐ ■	Bracelet extensible, 36 rondelles, plates
1328	☐ ■	Bracelet extensible, 36 rondelles, plates émaillées
1329	☐ ■	Bracelet extensible, cerisier
1330	☐ ■	Bracelet extensible, poussins
1331	☐ ■	Bracelet extensible, fougères
1332	☐ ■	Bracelet extensible, sophora
1333	☐ ■	Bracelet extensible, coqs
1334	☐ ■	Bracelet extensible, mésanges
1335	☐ ■	Bracelet extensible, palmettes
1336	☐ ■	Bracelet extensible, Renaissance
1337	☐ ■	Bracelet extensible, griffons
1338	☐ ■	Bracelet extensible, moineaux
1339	☐ ■	Bracelet extensible, soleils
1340	☐ ■	Bracelet extensible, muguets haut
1341	☐ ■	Bracelet extensible, muguets bas
1342	☐ ■	Bracelet extensible, Mauricette
1343	☐ ■	Bracelet extensible, créneaux

(Numbers 1344–1499 not listed)

Colliers [necklaces]

1500	■	Collier, grosses graines, boules ovales, 12 motifs
1501		
1502		
1503		
1504		
1505	☐ ■	Collier, lierre
1506		
1507		
1508		
1509	■	Collier, muguet, 20 motifs
1510	■	Collier, muguet, 24 motifs
1511	☐ ■	Collier, dahlias, 60 motifs
1512	☐ ■	Collier, zig-zag, 85 motifs

Design No.		French description	English description
1513	□ ■	Collier, boules (dahlias et rondelles plates), 23 boules	
1514	■	Collier, lotus, 22 motifs	
1515	■	Collier, fougères, 22 motifs	
1516	□	Collier, décors divers	

(Numbers 1517–1630 not listed)

Pendentifs [pendants]

1631	□	Pendentif ovale, sirènes	
1632	□	Pendentif ovale, fuchias	
1633			
1634			
1635			
1636			
1637			
1638	□	Pendentif ovale, figurine écharpe de face	
1639	□	Pendentif ovale, figurine écharpe de dos	
1640	□	Pendentif ovale, figurine ailée	
1641	□	Pendentif ovale, figurine se balançant	
1642	□	Pendentif rond, 2 figurine et fleurs	
1643	□	Pendentif rond, 3 papillons	
1644	□	Pendentif rond, 2 perruches	
1645	□	Pendentif coeur, figurine ailée	
1646	□	Pendentif coeur, cupidon	
1647	□	Pendentif carré, 2 figurines et fleurs	

(Numbers 1648–1660 not listed)

1661	□	Pendentif rond, 2 danseuses	
1662	□	Pendentif rond, figurine dans les fleurs	
1663	□	Pendentif, cigognes	

(Numbers 1664–2109 not listed)

2110	□	Candélabre, roitelets	*Listed under 'Divers'*

(Numbers 2111–2649 not listed)

Brûle parfums (à alcool) [scent burners]

2650	□ ■	Brûle parfums, papillons	*Plate 17*
2651	□ ■	Brûle parfums, sirènes	
2652	□	Brûle parfums, faune	
2653	□	Brûle parfums, carrousel	

(Numbers 2654–3001 not listed)

Coupes et assiettes [bowls and plates]

3001	□	Assiette, chasse chiens, émail	
3002	□	Assiette, 1 figurine et fleurs, émail	
3003	□ ■	Assiette, ondines	*Plate 81*
3004			
3005			
3006			*Bowl with sunflower design*

(Numbers 3007–3022 not listed)

3023	□ ■	Assiette, filix	

| Design
No. | French description | English description |

Design
No.   *French description*   *English description*

(Numbers 3024–3099 not listed)
3100 □   Coupe, bol fleur, émail
(Numbers 3101–3151 not listed)

Brocs et Carafes [jugs and decanters]

3152 □   Carafe, pyramidale
3153 □   Carafe, plate, 2 danseuses
3154
3155 ■   Carafe, reine marguerite
3155 ■   Carafe, reine marguerite avec bouchons verre
3156 ■   Carafe, masque
3156 ■   Carafe, masque avec bouchon verre
3156 ■   Carafe, masque avec bouchon argent
3157 □ ■   Carafe, aubèpine
3158 ■   Carafe, 6 figurines
3159
3160
3161 □ ■   Carafe, marguerites, bouchon pointe   *Plate 77*
3162
3163 □ ■   Carafe, coquilles
3164 □   Carafe, vrilles de vigne
3165 □ ■   Carafe, raisins
3166 □ ■   Carafe, plate, épines
3167
3168
3169 □ ■   Carafe, Dundee
3170 □   Carafe, bantam
3171 □   Carafe, padoue
3172 □   Carafe, faverolles
3173 □   Carafe, nippon
3174 □   Broc, bambou
3175 □   Carafe, coquelicot   *Plate 3176. (a)*
3176 □ ■   Broc, Jaffa
3177 □ ■   Broc, Blidah
3178 □ ■   Broc, Hespérides
3179 □ ■   Broc, Bahia
3180 □ ■   Broc, Sétubal
(Numbers 3181–3209 not listed)

Coupes et assiettes [bowls and plates]

3210 □ ■   Coupe, dahlias
3211
3212
3213 □ ■   Coupe, chicorée   *Plate 38*
(Numbers 3214–3222 not listed)
3223 ■   Coupe, gui No 1 (240mm)
3223 □   Coupe, gui No 1, émail
3224 ■   Coupe, gui No 2 (205mm)
3224 □   Coupe, gui No 2, émail
(Numbers 3225–3399 not listed)

Design No.	French description	English description

Gobelets et verres [goblets and glasses]

In this section ■ denotes a colour or enamel finish

3400	■	Gobelet, 6 figurines
3401	□ ■	Gobelet, raisins
3402	□ ■	Gobelet, épines
3403		
3404	□ ■	Gobelet, marguerites
3405	□	Gobelet, spirales
3406	□ ■	Gobelet, lotus
3407	□ ■	Gobelet, pavot
3408		
3409	■	Gobelet, coquelicot
3410	□ ■	Gobelet, Jaffa
3411	□ ■	Gobelet, Blidah
3412	□ ■	Gobelet, Hespérides No 1 (125mm)
3413	□ ■	Gobelet, Bahia
3414	□ ■	Gobelet, Sétubal
3415		
3416		
3417	□ ■	Gobelet, Hespérides No 2 (105mm)

(Numbers 3418–3459 not listed)

Jardinières

3460	□	Jardinière, acanthes	*Plate 148*
3461	□	Jardinière, Saint-Hubert	
3462	□	Jardinière, mésanges	

(Numbers 3463–3469 not listed)

Plateaux [trays]

3670	□ ■	Plateau rond, raisins
3671	□ ■	Plateau rond, épines
3672		
3673		
3674	□	Plateau rond, bantam
3675	□	Plateau rond, padoue
3676	□	Plateau rond, faverolles
3677	□	Plateau rond, nippon
3678	□	Plateau rond, bambou
3679	□	Plateau rond, coquelicot
3680	□ ■	Plateau rond, Jaffa
3681	□ ■	Plateau rond, Blidah
3682	□ ■	Plateau rond, Hespérides
3683	□ ■	Plateau rond, Bahia
3684	□ ■	Plateau rond, Sétubal

(Numbers 3685–3749 not listed)

Design No.	French description	English description

Gobelets et verres [goblets and glasses]
In this section ■ denotes a colour or enamel finish

3750 □ ■	Verre, frise personnages	
3751 ■	Verre à pied, grenouilles	*Known to have existed in 1922*
3752		
3753 ■	Verre à pied, bague chiens	
3754 ■	Verre à pied, bague lézards	
3755 ■	Verre à pied, chasse chiens No 1	
3756 ■	Verre à pied, chasse chiens No 2	
3757 □	Verre, vrilles de vigne	
3758 □	Verre, liseron	
3759		
3760		
3761		
3762		
3763		
3764 □	Verre, bantam	
3765 □	Verre, padoue	
3766 □	Verre, faverolles	
3767		
3768 □	Verre, bambou	
(Numbers 3769–5126 not listed)		
5127		*A wine glass on a squat base with a design of grapes; discontinued by 1932*
5128		*A wine glass on a squat base with a design of grapes; discontinued by 1932*
5129		*A wine glass on a squat base with a design of grapes; discontinued by 1932*
5130		*A wine glass on a squat base with a design of grapes; discontinued by 1932. Plate 172*
(Numbers 5131–5243 not listed)		
5244	Verre, nippon (77mm)	*Plate 65*

The 1932 catalogue
index of design numbers, listed
according to category of object

Ashtrays	275 *to* 320
Boxes and sweet-dishes	1 *to* 87
Bowls	375 *to* 413
Bracelets	1326 *to* 1343
Candelabra	2110
Car mascots and paperweights	801 *to* 804, 1121 *to* 1197
Clocks	725 *to* 736, 760 *to* 767
Dressing table sets	615 *to* 631
Glasses	3750 *to* 3768, 5127, 5244
Goblets	1121, 3400 *to* 3417
Hand blotters	150 *to* 157
Ink-wells	425 *to* 440
Jardinières	3460 *to* 3462
Jugs and carafes	3152 *to* 3180
Mirrors	675 *to* 686
Necklaces	1500 *to* 1516
Pendants	1634 *to* 1663
Picture frames	250 *to* 264
Plates	413 *to* 415, 3001 *to* 3023, 3100
Scent burners	2650 *to* 2653
Scent sprays	650 *to* 667
Seals	175 *to* 231
Statuettes	826 *to* 849, 1160, 1183
Surtouts (ornaments), illuminated plaques and sculptures, table decorations	1100 *to* 1111, 1149 *to* 1156, 1165 *to* 1167, 1169 *to* 1175, 1177 *to* 1180, 1199 *to* 1200
Tantaluses	1184 *to* 1190, 1201 *to* 1202
Trays	3670 *to* 3684
Vases	875 *to* 1076

Glossary

acanthe *acanthus*
aigrette *tuft*
aile *wing*
ailé(e) *winged*
aigle *eagle*
alcool *alcohol*
algue *seaweed*
amour(s) *cupid(s)*
ange(s) *angel(s)*
angle *side face*
anneau *ring*
anse *handle*
applique *light bracket, wallfitting*
armes *coat-of-arms*
artichaud *artichoke*
.assis(e) *seated*
aubèpine *hawthorn*

baie *berry*
balançant *balancing*
bambou *bamboo*
bas *bottom, low*
bavardant *chattering*
bélier *ram*
bergeronette *wagtail*
biche *doe*
bleuet *kingfisher*
bois *wood*
boîte *box*
bol à éponge *sponge bowl*
bonbonnière *sweet dish*
bordure *border*
bouchon *stopper*
boule *sphere, ball*
bras *arm(s)*
broc *jug*
brûle-parfums *scent-burner*
buvard *blotter*

cachet *seal*
camée *cameo*
canard *duck*
caravelle *sailing vessel*
cariatide *caryatid*

carré(e) *square*
carrousel *roundabout*
cavalier *horseman*
cendrier *ashtray*
cerise *cherry*
cerisier *cherry tree*
chardon *thistle*
chasse-chien *hound*
chat *cat*
cheval *horse*
chèvre *goat*
chicorée *chicory*
chien *dog*
chouette *owl*
cigale *cicada*
cigogne *stork*
coeur *heart*
coffret *box*
collier *necklace*
colombe *dove*
comète *comet*
coq *cock*
coquet *dainty*
coquille *shell*
cocquelicot *red poppy*
coupe *cup, bowl*
courge *pumpkin*
couvercle *cover*
créneaux *battlements*
cristal *crystal*
croisé *crossed*
cupidon *cupid*
cygne *swan*
cyprin *carp, goldfish*

daim *buck, deer*
danseuse *female dancer*
debout *upright*
dentelé *scalloped*
dindon *turkey*
divers *miscellaneous*
dormant *sleeping*
dos *back*
drapé(e) *draped*

écharpe *sash, scarf*
écureuil *squirrel*
émail *enamel*
émaillé(e) *enamelled*
enlacé(e) *intertwined*
encrier *inkwell*
enfant *child*
épervier *sparrowhawk*
épicéa *spruce fir*
épine *thorn*
escargot *snail*
étoile *star*
extensible *expanding*

farandole *a Provençal folk dance*
face *full face*
faucon *falcon*
faune *fawn*
fauvette *warbler*
fermé(es) *closed*
feu *fire*
feuille *leaf*
fier *proud*
flacon *flask*
fleur(s) *flower(s)*
fleurette *small flower*
fontaine *fountain*
fougère *fern*
frise *frieze*

garniture de toilette *dressing table set*
gland *tassel*
glissière *sliding*
glycine *wistaria*
gobelet *goblet*
grand(e) *big, tall*
grain *wheat*
gravé *cut, engraved*
grenouilles *frogs*
grillon *grass-hopper*
grimpereau(x) *creeper(s)*
gros(se) *large*
guêpe(s) *wasp(s)*
gui *mistletoe*
guirlande *garland*

hardi *bold*

haut *high*
hexagonale *six-sided*
hibou *owl*
hirondelle *swallow*
houppe *powder-puff*

inséparable(s) *love-bird(s)*

joint(es) *joined*
joueuse de flûte *flute player*

laiterons *hogweed*
lapin *rabbit*
lentille *lentil*
lévrier *greyhound*
lézard *lizard*
libellule *dragonfly*
lierre *ivy*
lièvre *hare*
lilas *lilac*
liseron *bindweed, convolvulus*
lutteur(s) *wrestler(s)*
lys *lily*

main *hand*
marguerite *daisy*
martin-pêcheur *kingfisher*
masque(s) *mask(s)*
mat *unpolished*
méplat *flat*
merle(s) *blackbird(s)*
mésange *tit*
miroir *mirror*
moineau(x) *sparrow(s)*
moineau moqueur *mynah bird*
monnaie du pape *honesty (flower)*
monture *mount*
moyen(ne) *medium*
muguet *lily-of-the-valley*
mûre *mulberry*
myosotis *forget-me-not*

naïade(s) *water-nymph(s)*
nain *dwarf*
néflier *medlar (tree)*
nénuphar *water-lily*
nid *nest*
nue *nude*

nymphe *nymph*

oeuf *egg (shaped)*
oiseau *bird*
ondine *water-nymph*
ormeau *young elm*
ouvert(es) *open*
ovale *oval*

palmette *palm frond*
panier *basket*
paon *peacock*
papillon *butterfly*
pâquerette *daisy*
parfum *perfume*
parot *poppy*
pêcheur *fisherman*
peigne(s) *comb(s)*
pendentif(s) *pendant(s)*
pendule *clock*
pendulette *small clock*
pervenche *periwinkle*
perle(s) *glass bead(s)*
perruche *parrot*
petit(e) *small*
phalène *moth, butterfly*
pied *foot*
pierrot *clown*
pinson *chaffinch*
pintade *guinea-fowl*
plateau *tray*
plat(e) *flat*
plume *feather*
poivre *pepper*
poli *polished*
polissoir *polishers*
pommier *apple tree*
porte-cigarette *cigarette-holder*
poudre *face powder*
poussin *chick*
poisson *fish*
primevère *primrose*
prune *plum*

raisin(s) *grape(s)*
reine *queen*
renard *fox*

renne *reindeer*
renoncule(s) *buttercup(s)*
roitelet *wren*
rond(e) *round*
rondelle(s) *small disc(s)*
rosace *rose*
rossignol *nightingale*

salamandre *salamander*
sanglier *wild boar*
satiné *frosted*
sauge *sage*
sauterelle *grasshopper*
scarabée *beetle*
serre-livre(s) *book-end(s)*
seul *single*
sirène *mermaid*
socle *base*
soie *silk*
soleil *sun*
souci *marigold*
souris *mouse*
sournois *artful*
spirale *spiral*
surtout *table centre-piece*

taillé *cut*
taureau *bull*
telline *shell*
tête *head*
tournesol *sunflower*
tortue *tortoise*
tourbillon *whirlpool*
tourterelle *turtledove*
trépied *tripod*

vague(s) *wave(s)*
vasque *bowl*
verre *glass*
victoire *victory*
vigne *vine*
vitesse *speed*
voilé(e) *veiled*
volubilis *convolvulus*
vrille(s) *tendril(s)*

zéphyr *breeze*

List of illustrations

28. Pierrefonds (990): white glass vase with satin body and polished handles.
29. Eucalyptus (936): a heavily moulded vase in satin white glass.
30. Rampillon (991): a small opalescent vase with a hand-stained floral design.
31. Tourbillons (973): heavily moulded vase with enamelled high relief.
32. Small highly polished vase with a brown stained background.
33. Ceylan (905): vase with pairs of birds in lightly polished relief against a satin background.
34. Coqs et plumes (1033): vase with polished design of cockerels in high relief against a tinted satin background.
35. A monumental vase, blown into a vast mould, perhaps with the aid of compressed air.
36. Danaïdes (972): vase with design of nymphs pouring water.
37. Archers (893): vase with polished relief against satin background.
38. Coupe Chicorée (3213): salad bowl in white glass with satin relief; fruit bowl in frosted glass with polished base; clear glass salad bowl with dandelion design in satin finish.
39. Eléphants (411): bowl with elephants in intaglio.
40. Detail of plate 39.
41. Madagascar (403): bowl in opalescent, satin glass with masks in high relief.
42. Detail of plate 41.
43. A completely clear vase designed to complement a dinner service.
44. Spirales (1060): opalescent vase with blue staining on the raised relief against a satin background.
45. Prunes (1037): vase with thick relief in satin and polished highlights.
46. Cerises (1035): vase presented in 1977 to Princess Grace of Monaco.
47. Heavy vase with a pattern of stylized flowers against background of crushed ice.
48. Heavy moulded vase with a wave design in polished relief against a background of crushed ice.
49. Ferrières (1019): opalescent vase, with polished relief against a greeny-blue satin background.
50. Highly polished opalescent vase with a design of petals.
51. Tournai (956): vase with satin background with leaves in polished relief.
52. Covered vase with satin finish and a border of devil masks round the neck.
53. Amiens (1023): a clear glass vase with handles in a satin finish.
54. Chamaraude (974): clear, slightly topaz vase, with brown staining on the satin handles.
55. Honfleur (944): a small fine vase with lightly stained handles.
56. Ornis (976): vase; wide variations in thickness give the base and birds an opalescent appearance.
57. Béliers (904): polished glass vase with satin handles.
58. Fruit bowl on white glass, hand-stained in green.

59. Marguerite: vase with clear glass flowers against a greeny-blue background.
60. Dahlias (938): satin, white glass vase with flower design and enamelled stamens.
61. Three fruit bowls.
62. Poissons (925): opaque and lightly polished vase, with a satin tinted background.
63. Brilliant blue bowl with a design of peacock feathers.
64. Sophora (977): vase with polished relief on a satin background.
65. Verres Nippon (5244): two wine glasses from an extensive range of tableware; decanter in polished glass, stopper with satin finish and polished relief.
66. Artist's impression of the dining room in the Lalique pavilion at the 1925 Exposition des Arts Décoratifs et Industriels Modernes.
67. A decanter and one of four different sizes of wine glass from a set designed in the late twenties.
68. Bourgueil: decanter and glasses in clear glass with relief in satin finish. This set was first made after 1932 and has been continued by Cristal Lalique.
69. White glass decanter, part of a set designed before 1925.
70. Attractive decanter, part of a set, in clear moulded glass with a border round the neck in a satin finish.
71–73. Tableware presented by the city of Paris to King George VI and Queen Elizabeth in 1938.
74. A lemonade set in amber glass.
75. Jaffa (3176): a white glass lemonade set with satin finish.
76. Candlestick in frosted glass with flowers in gold enamel.
77. Marguerites (3161): white glass with satin design.
78. Set of tableware in clear glass with green staining on the satin relief.
79. Marienthal: plate in white frosted glass.
80. A white glass bowl with frosted border showing traces of blue staining.
81. Ondines (3003): white glass plate with frosted relief.
82. Lys (382): clear glass bowl supported by three opalescent lilies.
83. Archer (1126): car mascot in clear glass with satin-finished intaglio design.
84. Rhinocéros (1195): satin finish with grey hand-staining on a clear glass base.
85. 5 Chevaux (1122), a car mascot commissioned by Citroën in 1925.
86. Aigle (428): car mascot in white glass.
87. Faucon (1124): polished clear glass car mascot.
88. Hirondelle (1143): polished clear glass car mascot with satin base.
89. Comète (1123): clear glass car mascot.
90. Grande libellule (1145): car mascot with satin finished body and polished relief and wings.
91. Epsom (1153): car mascot in white glass with satin finish and polished mane.

117. Epines (593): white glass scent bottle with green stained background, part of a dressing table set.
118. White glass scent bottle with satin finish, hand-stained with green.
119. Marguerites (69): polished clear glass bowl with brown staining. Scent bottle in white glass with satin finish and polished relief.
120. Caravelle *surtout* presented by the city of Paris to the British King and Queen in 1938: it was identical to the model listed in the 1932 catalogue (1169).
121. Ceiling light in white glass with satin finish and polished relief.
122. Detail of ceiling light reproduced in plate 121.
123. Acanthus: ceiling light in white glass with satin finish and polished relief.
124. Illustration from *La Sculpture Décorative Moderne* (Editions d'Art Charles Moreau, Paris) showing Trois paons *surtout* (1110), Grande veilleuse table lamp and Deux cavaliers surtout (1109).
125. Gros poisson, vagues (1100): white glass fish on bronze base. Gros poisson, algues (1101): white glass fish on bronze base.
126. Display at Maison Rouard, a Paris gallery where Lalique frequently exhibited his glass.
127. Iron gates designed by Bellery Desfontaines in 1913, incorporating two heavy glass medallions by Lalique.
128. Photograph from Guillaume Janneau's book, *Modern Glass*, showing the Arcade des Champs Elysées; Lalique designed the fountain and glass lanterns.
129. Façade of the Worth shop in Cannes, executed in black marble and illuminated glass in 1926.
130. Panel, identical to those used by Oswald Milne in the redecoration of Claridge's in 1932.
131. Reredos in the Lady Chapel of St Matthew's Church, St Helier, Jersey; illuminated glass with satin finish in a stainless steel frame.
132. Glass font designed by Lalique for St Matthew's; satin and clear glass.
133. Detail of a window in St Matthew's.
134. Detail of a pillar at the side of the main altar of St Matthew's.
135. Interior of the Côte d'Azur Pullman-car for which Lalique designed the partition panels.
136. Artist's impression of the first class dining room of the liner *Normandie*, launched in 1935 (from a special edition of *L'Illustration*, June 1932).
137. Door handle, in the form of a bee, with satin finish and polished relief.
138. Statuette issued by the Compagnie des Wagon-lits to commemorate the inauguration of the Côte d'Azur Pullman-car in 1929.
139. Amour assis (3): white glass box with satin finish and traces of blue staining.
140. Naïade (832): opalescent statuette with satin finish and polished relief.
141. Sirène (831): opalescent statuette with satin finish and polished base.
142. Naïade (221): white statuette with satin design in intaglio.
143. Mûres (156): white glass blotter with satin finish and polished relief.

144. Nue (836): white glass statuette with satin finish, on wooden base.
145. Moyenne nue (830): white glass statuette with satin finish.
146. Naïades (764): clock in opalescent glass with satin finish; the face is hand-painted ivory.
147. Inséparables (765): clock in opalescent glass with satin finish.
148. Acanthes (3460): jardinière in white glass with satin finish and traces of blue staining.
149. Seal with satin finish and grey hand-staining.
150. Deux oiseaux (677): back of a hand-mirror in white glass with satin finish and lightly polished relief.
151. 'Replique' scent bottle in gilt metal and satin glass, worn as a pendant. Enamelled signature.
152. Pendant with satin finish and lightly polished relief.
152. Pendant with a frosted glass surface, giving the appearance of rock crystal; the fishes are in blue enamel. The silver chain is not contemporary.
154. Pendant with satin finish and polished reverse.
155. Pendant with satin finish and polished relief.
156. Pendant in blue glass with satin finish depicting wasps.
157. Pendant in opalescent glass, with design of lilies of the valley.
158. Pendant in opalescent glass, with design of lilies.
159. Blue glass pendant with satin surface and lightly polished relief.
160. Dinard (78): white glass box with satin finish.
161. Cyprins (42): box in opalescent glass.
162. Black glass box with patinated design on the lid in the form of a chrysanthemum.
163. Roger (75): box in white glass with black enamel relief.
164. Box in frosted green glass with polished relief and silver scarab hinges and clasp.
165. *Cire perdue* study of two sinister animals. Lalique has used his fingerprints to create the texture of the light grey surface.
166. *Cire perdue* vase with a design of eucalyptus leaves in opaque, rough textured glass.
167. *Cire perdue* vase in opaque, rough textured glass with hazlenut and leaf motifs.
168. Degas (66): box in white glass with satin finish.
169. Vase gobelet, 6 figurines (903): the figures are in heavy relief with a satin finish and traces of blue staining.
170. Magnificent *cire perdue* bowl in opaque, rough textured white glass with four grotesque fish masques.
171. Saint-Denis (388): a fine example of an object created by hand blown and power press techniques. The stem is partly enamelled.
172. Page from a 1927 issue of *The Studio*. The vase is Grimpereaux (987).

Books:

BATTERSBY, MARTIN: *The World of Art Nouveau.* Arlington Books, London, 1968
BATTERSBY, MARTIN: *The Decorative Twenties.* Studio Vista, London, 1971
BATTERSBY, MARTIN: *The Decorative Thirties.* Studio Vista, London, 1969
GEOFFROY, GUSTAV: *René Lalique.* E. Mary, Paris, 1922
JANNEAU, GUILLAUME: *Modern Glass.* The Studio, London, 1931
LALIQUE, MARC AND MARIE-CLAUDE: *Lalique.* Societé Lalique, Paris
McCLINTON, KATHERINE: *Lalique for Collectors.* Charles Scribner's Sons, New York, 1975
STUDIO, THE: *Year Book of Decorative Art,* 1914
STUDIO, THE: *Year Book of Decorative Art,* 1928

Catalogues:

Cristal Lalique catalogue
'Daily Mail' Ideal Home Exhibition catalogue, 1931
Gulbenkian Collection catalogue
'Lalique at C.V.P.', catalogue 1974
'Lalique, Light and Decoration', catalogue. Breves Galleries, London, 1928
R. Lalique & Company catalogue, 1932

Magazines:

Architectural Review, The; February 1928
Art et Décoration; July 1902
Country Life; June 1974
L'Illustration; 18 December 1939
Mobilier et Décoration; January 1927
Studio, The; July 1902
Studio, The; February 1931
Studio Magazine of Beauty, The; September 1938

Acknowledgements

OF THE MANY PEOPLE who have advised me in the preparation of this book, I should particularly like to thank Noël Tovey for his constant and enthusiastic support; Richard Sachs, who edited the book and assisted me in my research; and Marc Lalique and Marie-Claude Lalique, whose visit to an exhibition of René Lalique's glass which my wife and I assembled in 1974 gave us both immense encouragement. I have also received valuable help from Christopher Baker, Coty Ltd, Philippe Garner, Martin Hunt, John Jesse, Neil Lorrimer, David Sarel and Alan Wrangles; and I wish to acknowledge my considerable obligation to Katharine Morrison McClinton, whose pioneering study of Lalique's 1932 catalogue (*Lalique for Collectors*, Charles Scribner's Sons, New York, 1975) has provided me with much essential information. Finally, I am much indebted to three admirable books by Mrs Martin Battersby – *The World of Art Nouveau* (Arlington Books, London, 1968), *The Decorative Thirties* (Studio Vista, London, 1969) and *The Decorative Twenties* (Studio Vista, 1971) – on which I have relied extensively for my references to the work of Lalique's predecessors and contemporaries.

Blacker Calmann Cooper Ltd would like to thank the following for kindly allowing the objects in their collections to be reproduced: Her Majesty Queen Elizabeth the Queen Mother (plates 12, 71, 72 and 73); John Jesse (plate 85); John McCall (plate 18); Heather Arnold (plate 19); Noël Tovey (plates 92, 169, 166 and 169); the Corning Glass Museum (plate 163). They would also like to thank those who provided the photographs for the book: Neil Lorrimer, John Vaughan of *Harpers and Queen* (plates 130–133); Intraflug AG (plate 134).

Index

Page numbers in *italic* refer to illustrations